WHEN
SCIENCE
MEETS
SPIRITUALITY

WHEN SCIENCE MEETS SPIRITUALITY

Ramakrishna Vijayacharya Hosur

Retired Senior Professor
Department of Chemical Sciences
Tata Institute of Fundamental Research (TIFR)
Homi Bhabha Road, Colaba, Mumbai

Formerly Director
UM-DAE Centre for Excellence in Basic Sciences
University of Mumbai, Kalina, Mumbai

Currently Distinguished Visiting Professor
Department of Bioscience and Bioengineering
Indian Institute of Technology (IIT) Bombay
Powai, Mumbai

न हि ज्ञानेन सदृशं पवित्रमिह विद्यते।

There is nothing as pure as knowledge

ॐ पूर्णमदः पूर्णमिदं पूर्णात्पूर्णमुदच्यते।
पूर्णस्य पूर्णमादाय पूर्णमेवावशिष्यते॥
ॐ शान्तिः शान्तिः शान्तिः ॥

Isha Upanishad, Brihadaranyaka Upanishad

Aum! That is infinite, and this (universe) is infinite.
The infinite proceeds from the infinite.
(Then) taking the infinitude of the infinite (universe),
It remains as the infinite alone.
Aum! Peace! Peace! Peace!

नारायणाय परिपूर्ण गुणार्णवाय ।
विश्वोदयस्थितिलयोन्नियति प्रदाय ।
ज्ञानप्रदाय विबुधासुरसौख्य दुःख ।
सत्करणाय विततताय नमो नमस्ते ।

Mahabharat Tatparya Nirnaya

Oh Lord Narayana, I bow you again and again; you are like an ocean of infinite auspicious qualities [like knowledge and bliss], the originator and cause for the creation, sustenance, annihilation and primary instigator for the entire universe, bestower of knowledge [for uttamas, madhyamas and adhamas according to their yogyata], the highest cause for the inherent joy of gods (good people), inherent sorrow of demons (evil people) [by implication a mixture of joys and sorrow to the middle kind] and you pervade the universe in a unique and extra-ordinary way.

Published by
Saptarishi Publications
Second Floor 2/15 Ansari Road,
Daryaganj New Delhi 110002

ISBN 978-81-962157-5-0
© Saptarishi

First Edition 2024
MRP ₹400

Editor: Neel Sarovar Bhavesh
Sketch by Maitrayee Majumder
Cover and Typesetting by Ayush Kumar
Printed by Sagar Printer, Delhi

Contents

Foreword

I believe both science and spirituality share a search for the truth and for understanding reality. By learning from science about aspects ofreality where its understanding may be more advanced, I believe that spirituality enriches its own worldview.

Science and spirituality are different but with complementary approaches to seeking the truth. There is much each may learn from the other and together they may contribute to expanding the horizon of human knowledge and wisdom. Indeed, I encourage my Buddhist colleagues to undertake the study of science, so that its insights can be integrated into the Buddhist worldview.

Within ancient India's spiritual traditions there is a deep understanding of the mind's capacity for transformation from a negative state to a state of tranquil and wholesome purity. For Buddhism especially, given its primary interest in questions of ethics, spirituality, and overcoming suffering, understanding consciousness, is ofgreat importance. I feel strongly that coming to a scientific understanding of consciousness will be most significant.

Today, in the first quarter of the twenty-first century, science and spirituality have the potential to come closer than ever, and to embark upon collaborative endeavours that will have far-reaching potential to help humanity meet the challenges before us.

It is also my hope that we can bring our spirituality, the full richness and simple wholesomeness of our basic human values, to bear upon the course ofscience and the direction oftechnology in human society so they may contribute to the betterment of humanity.

In this book entitled 'When Science Meets Spirituality', Dr. Ramakrishna V. Hosur explains how a scientist like him can continue to follow a spiritual path without compromising his scientific beliefs. I commend him for his candour and hope readers will find it interesting and helpful.

12 September 2024

Foreword

"When Science Meets Spirituality" is a topic of great interest to most people, which continues to be debated fiercely in both scientific and spiritual circles. Often, many specialists think that the two topics, science and spirituality, are too distinctly different and have nothing in common. While the science fraternity alleges spirituality to be just blind faith, the spiritualists, on the other hand, claim that spirituality starts where science ends. The author has elegantly addressed these viewpoints.

The book progresses systematically in building up the narrative by first showing the glorious developments in science; then it establishes the fundamental concepts in the spirituality of Consciousness, Super-soul, Order, and such other entities, which are not directly amenable to experimental investigations, by navigating through the common experiences in life. The author then consolidates this further by showing ancient wisdom regarding the creation of the universe, order in the Universe, and health aspects. The author then delves deeper into the philosophical concepts. In all of this discussion, original Sanskrit statements are cited to establish the authenticity, but their meanings in English are also included for easy comprehension. The spiritual texts also give prescriptions for a happy life, which we may call the 'Philosophy of Life.'

Overall, this forms an excellent reading for an inquisitive mind and helps remove many misconceptions.

—Prof. Anand Ranganathan, Scientist and Author

Preface

This book is an outcome of my experiences in life. I have practiced for the last 50 years, and continue to practice science as a profession. While the journey has been enjoyable, it had its own ups and downs, anxious moments, successes and failures as measured by the yardsticks of science prevailing. These were also intermingled with personal ups and downs. At the same time, the fundamental principles and concepts of spirituality to which I got introduced as a child, continuously guided me and brought solace on occasions of despair. In the end it has been a great lesson for getting peace.

This experience has helped me in providing solace to many colleagues and students at the time of their anxious moments. Inspired by this

I have ventured here to put down some salient aspects relating to the practice of science and also of spirituality. I do not claim to be great expert in either of the fields, and in fact, it is hard to find all the expertise in one individual; most often, miseries arise as a result of ignorance and egos. But even the minimal knowledge covering the fundamental principles will be extremely helpful to get over ignorance, uncertainties and accept life as it comes and thus remain calm and peaceful.

The book is basically organised in seven chapters. The chapters are arranged systematically, beginning with classical thinking as a scientist and proceed towards spirituality, learning from ancient wisdom where the two fields of science and spirituality were not separated. The sixth chapter presents a broad protocol for human behavior to be happy and peaceful. The final chapter contains some important quotes from the scriptures for getting peace. I have used at many places original quotes which are in Sanskrit language, but have included their meanings in a simplified manner so as to drive home the message contained therein. I have also derived substantial information available in the public domain using internet and incorporated them at several places. The contents reflect my own thoughts as I have grasped them from reading the various texts, which include scientific works and spiritual texts. The presentation is restricted to concepts only, rather than going into elaborate technical details, so as to enable lay people to assimilate the subject matter easily, and accordingly adjust their lifestyles. The basic message I want to convey here is that science and spirituality are not separable, are two faces of the same coin, and this perception enhances each other, which in the end leads to better quality of each individual's life and better harmony in the society.

—Ramakrishna V Hosur

Acknowledgements

I am immensely grateful to my parents, grandparents, brothers, sisters, maternal uncles, my wife and her family, my children, and my students throughout my career, for being able to produce this work. I am particularly indebted to my elder brothers Dr Madhusoodan V Hosur and Shri Mohan V Hosur for very critical comments, critical reading and suggestions to improve the text. I am thankful to Dr Neel Sarovar Bhavesh for taking the initiative to publish this book. I am also grateful to my publisher Mr Aman Ujjwal for publishing my manuscript.

Chapter 1

Modern Science Perspective of the World

Summary: This chapter provides the views prevalent in the current world of science and technology. The belief among the youth and a large fraction of the educated elite is that everything happening in the universe is understandable in terms of the physical laws. A brief description of the origin and evolution of the Universe, and life in it, as we perceive today is provided. The tendency is to discard the preexisting dogma about existence of abstract entities such as Soul and God.

UNDOUBTEDLY, scientific pursuits have enhanced the comfort level in all our lives. There is no debate that pursuit of science produces new knowledge, which in turn leads to new technologies that impact our lifestyles. Science as we witness today has evolved, approximately, over the last 400 years, the most dramatic results having come only in the last century. Scientific thoughts and theories continue to evolve, as more and more data and observations accumulate. A generally accepted belief in scientific pursuit is that every theory represents truth until it is falsified by new data. Another strong belief is that there is perfect order in the universe, which is evident from the fact the laws of nature remain unchanged and everything that happens is in accordance with those laws.

The Universe evolves under the governing principle, 'attain a state of high stability or low potential energy'. The evolution of Universe started from an infinitely tiny point of infinitely high density of energy after the so-called 'big bang' which happened some 13.9 billion (another estimate is a range, 15-20 billion) years ago, as per the present understanding. The event, 'big-bang' is considered to be the beginning of 'time'

Initially, it was all waves or fluctuations representing Energy. Whatever were the laws of physics then (which we do not know), were different from the laws we see now. Thinking

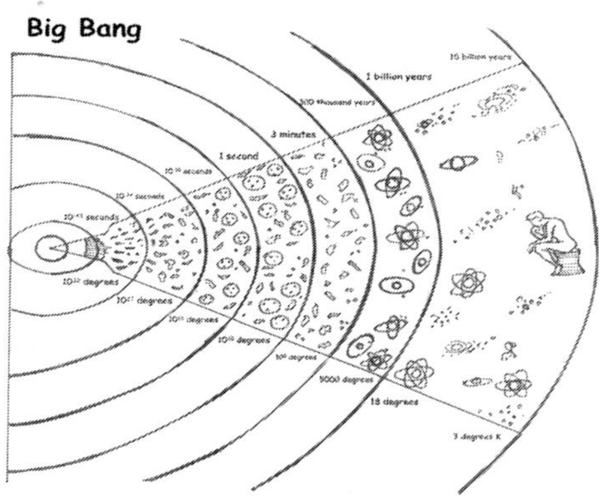

in terms of the current laws, the temperature at that point was 10^{32} degrees Celsius. The big bang caused a rapid expansion which resulted in some cooling which in turn resulted in some condensation of energy into elementary particles. 'Quarks' were the most fundamental particles which were, however, unstable. The hot particles would collide because of the extremely high density and reconvert into energy. This process occurred repeatedly, and as the expansion and cooling continued more and more stable particles remained. This includes particles such as 'electron', 'proton', 'neutron' and many more. Quarks became integral constituent parts of these particles. The stable particles had certain intrinsic characteristics, which were called as Charge, Spin,

Momentum, Mass etc. For example, electron has a so-called negative charge and a proton has a so-called positive charge. There are other particles with their own characteristic properties.

The particles would interact with each other to reach a state of low energy (stability) and certain laws as we know today emerged naturally on this count. For example, particles with positive and negative charges would attract each other, and particles with charge of the same sign would repel each other. We called them with certain names such as 'electrostatic interaction', 'Coulomb's law', "van der Waals law', 'nuclear interaction' etc. Atoms were formed by such interactions. Atoms interacted to form molecules, and molecules condensed to form visible materials or matter.

The matter condensed further and this resulted in the formation of stars, galaxies, planets etc. in different regions of space. The expansion continued in such a way that every object was moving away from every other object, just like the spots on a balloon that move apart as the balloon gets blown. Again, these objects acquired certain properties by virtue of interactions among the constituent matter elements. Thus, stars would emit radiation while planets would not have that ability. The temperature in the stars was very high and that in the planets was very low.

The process of condensation to reach a stable configuration would involve an attractive force which was termed, 'Gravitation'. By natural selection, this followed a certain mathematical law, which we call as 'Law of Gravitation' – the Gravitational force is inversely proportional to the square of the distance between two objects and directly proportional to the product of the masses of the two objects. This was responsible for the so-called 'order' in the Universe. Planets would get associated with stars and revolve around them resulting in dynamic stability of the system.

In all of the above a 'Conservation Principle' was implicit. Laws of motion of matter on the planets and the laws of thermodynamics emerged to explain the physical and chemical phenomena that were observed.

As per the current theories, the total of visible matter does not fully account for the amount of energy in the Universe – in fact it accounts for only 5% of the total energy. It is hypothesised that the rest of it exists, partly as 'dark matter' and partly as 'dark energy (almost 70%)'. It is thought that the dark energy is responsible for the accelerated expansion of the Universe, as per the interpretation of the current experimental observations. Further research would throw more light on these with regard to the validity of the hypothesis and the related interpretations.

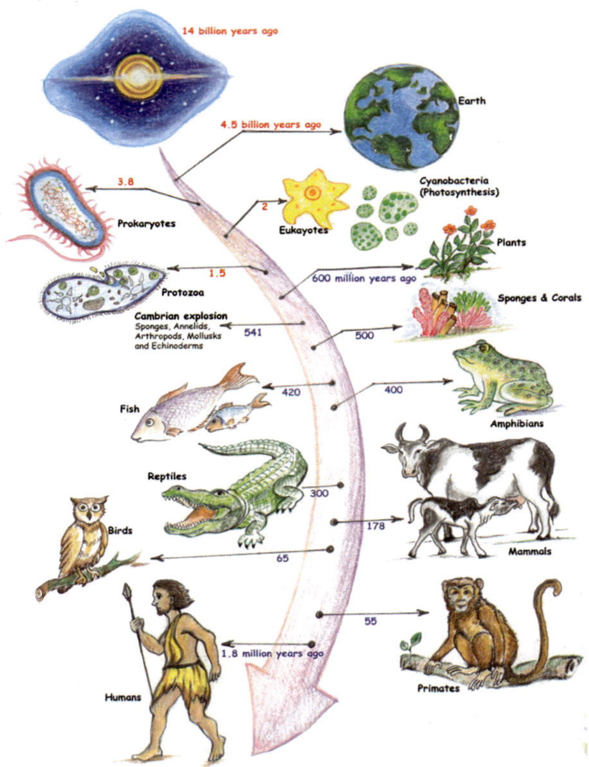

The most popular view of origin of life on earth is: Life emerged on the earth and perhaps on some other planets (which we do not know still), as a consequence of interaction between molecules (matter) by the process of natural selection and survival of the most stable state.

First, cells (small closed impermeable entities) were formed for maximizing efficacy of interactions. Intracellular interactions between molecules caused duplication and multiplication of the cells. Cell - Cell interactions resulted in organisms and higher species with ever increasing order. It is estimated that today there are about 8.7 million different species on the earth; some estimates give a range, 7.4-10.0 million. Most complex and coordinated interactions among the various components resulted in the emergence of the so-called 'intellect', which implies ability to think, store information, plan actions etc. The humans are the highest-level intellectual species. This intellect resulted in Technology, ability to change, develop etc.

Pure and applied Science

The pace of development and generation of new knowledge and concepts quickly became so vast that no single individual would be capable of acquiring expertise over all the fields, and a systematic classification emerged naturally to facilitate a more organised growth. In this context, scientific knowledge got conveniently broadly classified into 'pure science' and 'applied science'. In turn, pure science got categorized into four subjects, namely, Physics, Chemistry, Biology, and Mathematics; applied science which basically is the outcome of innovations based on pure science, included subjects of engineering/ technology.

Physics deals with properties and dynamics in the inanimate world. Newton's laws of motion, law of gravitation according to which two objects with mass attract each other and this governs planetary motions in space, Astronomy and Astrophysics which help understand our solar system, stars, galaxies etc, Earth Sciences or Geology which are related to earth-quakes, volcanos, etc, properties of materials which are used in our daily life, energy generation are some common examples.

Chemistry deals with interactions among the various inanimate objects. Formation of molecules from atoms, synthesis of various compounds used in items of daily use such as soaps, toothpastes, paints, plastics, clothes, paper, cosmetics, inks, drugs, etc are some of the common examples.

Biology deals with behaviour and functioning of living objects. How does a single living cell from a mother develop into a full human being? How do plants synthesise food? What causes diseases and how can they be cured by use of drugs? How does the food, we eat, get metabolized to form blood, flesh, bone etc? What is memory? What is reproduction and why do the off-springs resemble their parents in some manner? And so on.

Finally, Mathematics provides the abstract concepts which are useful in all the other three fields. Number system, algebra, calculus, analysis, statistics, are some of the most familiar terms. Computer science, often clubbed together with mathematics, has revolutionized various operations, enhanced computational speeds, enhanced precision and control of parameters in various experiments. In each of these there were further division into many different specialised branches.

Likewise, the applied sciences were also further divided. Engineering areas were: civil engineering which dealt with constructions of buildings, roads, bridges, dams, and the like; mechanical engineering which dealt with building machines; electrical engineering which dealt with matters related to electricity, magnetism; chemical engineering which dealt with synthesis of materials on large scale; aviation and aeronautical engineering which dealt with manufacture of aircrafts; satellite engineering which dealt with building of satellites, spacecrafts, rockets, etc; agriculture which dealt with cultivation, food production; computer engineering which dealt with building computers, development of algorithms for various applications, machine learning, artificial intelligence etc. Again, in each of these there were further divisions into many different specialised branches.

Life Sciences and health care

Physiology and medicine were subjects related to health and development of living species which included insects, animals and humans. Again, in each of these there were further divisions into many different specialised branches. Primarily some related to anatomical aspects of the bodies, others related to aspects inside the bodies. Technological developments in engineering fields were intimately networked with requirements in physiology and medicine. For example, imaging techniques so important for understanding the changes in the interiors of the physical bodies were necessarily outcomes of mechanical, electrical, computer technologies.

Pharmaceutical science which belongs to the realm of medicine is an extremely important branch which deals with diseases, drugs, and therapies. By and large, the diseases are diagnosed on the basis of specific symptoms and after a variety of tests. In the modern times drugs for specific diseases are approved by competent agencies for usage after extensive clinical tests and quality controls. The approved drugs are manufactured in large quantities by chemical synthesis by pharmaceutical industries and here the chemical engineering concepts play crucial roles.

The above very brief description of different aspects of science is simply illustrative to help appreciate the enormity of the developments in the world, and I have no intention, nor is it necessary here, to be exhaustive with regard to developments either in pure science or in applied science fields.

The process of scientific investigation involves primarily three components: (i) direct experimentation, (ii) logic and (iii) established fault-free literature. Different approaches will be used depending upon the nature of the subject under investigation. In the scientific world, all the above three methods are related, direct experimentation being the most powerful, which then leads to logic and literature. Scientific experimentation deals almost invariably with material world and tries to explain everything happening in this universe, in terms of material transformations, whether it be in the living objects or in the inanimate objects.

Outcomes of scientific research are highly quantifiable and can be subjected to serious scrutiny by others in the field. If a scientist has made an observation, the experimental details and the results of the experiments have to be truthfully reported for others to follow, and to repeat the experiments, if they wish, to verify the correctness of the experiments and the derived results. In scientific endeavour, the experiments are, often, curiosity driven, and the social benefits may not be immediately apparent. Innovations on these results lead to technological advancements which would benefit the society.

Technological innovations such as, Television, Telephones, Airplanes, Locomotives, Wireless Transmission, Mobiles, Medical Equipment, Artificial Intelligence (AI), satellites, internet, to name a few, have changed the lifestyles of all beings. These have provided enormously powerful tools for communication, transportation, healthcare, reduced efforts required for accomplishing huge tasks, simplified daily activities, improved infrastructures, enhanced safety measures, helped disaster management during natural calamities and many more. Humans have even landed on the Moon and explored the Mars planet.

Research in all the areas continues and the more we learn, the more we realise that there is so much more we do not know. New questions arise, earlier concepts get changed, new theories emerge, and we do not see an end to this process. Sometimes, this is considered as the strength of scientific pursuit and reflects openness in the thinking process. However, in such a scenario a question arises: is there anything like absolute and unchangeable truth? In turn, since our convictions in modern science impact our lifestyles seriously, the uncertainty leads to confusions as to what is right action? what is wrong action? what is good food? what is bad food? what is ethical? what is unethical? etc.

Is there a God?

All the above incredible accomplishments which were unimaginable few decades ago have infused in the minds of the intellectuals, the thought that everything that happens on this earth and in the Universe is understandable in due course of time, as Science and Technology keep evolving.

Mankind has achieved incredible feats

Everything here is material or energy in nature. There is no need to invoke the existence of God.

The incredible accomplishments have also made some disastrous impacts. Human ambitions have been the root cause of such disasters. Weapons of mass destruction, lead to competitions for acquiring more and more at the cost of others, race for superiority, territorial expansion ambitions, wars, one-upmanship, tendencies to dominate over other individuals or other nations with no concern for ethical values or humanitarian considerations. After the Nuclear Bomb explosion in Japan in 1945 during the world war II, which killed millions of people, Robert Oppenheimer, the inventor of the bomb said to the President of America who had ordered that disastrous action, "Mr President, I have blood on my hands". Creating more and more wealth has become the most central theme of all human pursuits. The underlying belief is that wealth can enable any person to acquire whatever he desires.

Chapter 2

Spirituality

Summary: This chapter introduces, in a narrative style using common daily life experiences, the concepts in Spirituality. There are many abstract entities such as 'soul', 'super-soul', 'order', 'dharma', 'adharma' which are not accessible to direct experimentation. But their existence cannot be denied. These play crucial roles in our understanding of our existence and our relation to the world or the universe. This has been a topic pondered over by many eminent people, but in the present context of relation with modern science, I have documented views of some highly respected scientists who lived during the last century.

SPIRITUALITY is often identified with religion. Its scope is in fact much wider, as we will see later. A question that has been mostly encountered in the minds of humans is: has spirituality, which has been the general norm in life for several centuries, any role to play in our lives today? It is a very common phrase among modern youth and many intellectuals that Spirituality is all *blind faith*, whereas Science is based on solid experimental evidences; therefore, Spirituality has to be done away with. Some of them even feel ashamed to talk about spirituality. They look down upon persons talking about spirituality, labeling them as old fashioned, uneducated, and ignorant of modern scientific and technological advances.

Faith

- In every family, a child, small or grown up, knows who his/her parents are, although he/she has no direct proof by himself/herself for the same.
- When you teach your child various things by simplification, some of which may not be entirely correct in your own judgement, the child accepts all of them as truths.
- When you advise your close friend to

approach a particular Doctor for treatment of a particular disease, the friend accepts it and seeks the suggested advice without any hesitation.

One can list many more such day-to-day life experiences, which everyone will come across, and all of these go to prove that 'faith' is an essential element of life. No one on this planet knows everything about everything, not even everything about something, and hence one cannot live without having faith on words of some other people. Otherwise. you will end-up in an infinite regress – to verify a particular statement, A goes to B, B goes to C, C goes to D, and so on, which can become unending. Faith relies on trust, and who is trustworthy will be determined by whether the person referred to is your well-wisher or a highly knowledgeable person by public experience.

Faith, by nature represents truth, until it is proven untrue. Therefore, faith has an important presence even in science as well. An individual undertakes an investigation only when he gets a doubt about something which he has believed in. Investigation on the validity of an information happens primarily by three methods: (i) direct experimentation, (ii) logic and (iii) established fault-free literature. Different approaches will be used depending upon the nature of the subject under investigation. In the scientific world, all the above three methods are related, direct experimentation being the most powerful, which then leads to logic and literature. Scientific experimentation deals almost invariably with material world and tries to explain everything happening in this universe, in terms of material transformations, whether it be in the living objects or in the inanimate objects. Invariably, any particular scientist has expertise in one particular area, but he believes in the experimental data and their interpretation in a different field by another scientist, and that is again a matter of faith. In fact, the very statement that any theory or interpretation is true until it is falsified is itself a reflection on role of faith in scientific pursuits.

Thus, one has to accept that faith by nature is blind, no matter what field one is concerned with, spirituality or science, and represents truth temporarily, until it is falsified by other evidences. Are there entities in

this world whose existence can never be falsified? Those entities would represent absolute truth.

Abstract entities

Now the question is: is every observation in one's life accessible to direct experimental validation?

When I accomplish something, I say, I am happy. Who is this 'I'?

When I cut my finger, I say, I am hurt. Who is this 'I'?

When a person dies, the body is visible to everybody, but we say, He/she *was* so kind, He/She *was* a renowned scientist, He/She *was* an expert surgeon etc'. To the body, we say 'it', meaning it is just some material. The usage of past-tense, 'was', to describe the individual even though the body is still there, indicates that something which is clearly different from the body, has disappeared. What is that something?

Who experiences the emotions of happiness, sorrow, success, failure, anger, peace? Although the emotions may manifest in material changes in the body, which may not be visible directly, but may be probed by scientific tools, the experience itself goes in the account of some object, 'I',

'He', 'She' etc. This abstract entity cannot be identified with any material, but must reflect the existence of an entity, which is inside the body, yet different from the body or the mind (mind is integral part of the body). This is called the 'Soul' or the 'Atma', which is beyond the reach of direct experimentation. The Atma performs all its actions using the body.

Suppose you are fast asleep and there is nobody around you. At that time the Atma is not doing any work and is completely disconnected from the external world and even with his own body. Now, when you wake up at some time by yourself, how do you wake up? Someone else has to act on you, and who is that someone? When you wake up you get a feeling that 'I slept so well for so long'. Since your own mind was inactive for so long, the biological processes that may be going on in the body cannot produce the knowledge that touches the soul. Therefore, some other soul is keeping track of your status without your knowledge and he gives that knowledge to you at the end. Who is he?

The actions of an Atma can be classified as 'good' or 'bad', and the rewards are enjoyed by the Atma. 'Goodness' (called as Dharma) or

'Badness' (Adharma) of an action is again an abstract entity, because a particular action may be termed good or bad depending upon the situation.

Intuitively, disorder or chaos is more natural, but it is no denying that there is enormous Order in the Universe. The planetary system, the galaxies, the stars etc display perfect order and the various laws of physics define this order, some illustrative specific laws are: the law of gravitation, the law that like charges repel and opposite charges attract each other, the principle that materials always try to approach the state of lowest potential energy (PE), which is taken to represent a stable state, that a stable state is essential for performing a function etc. How did these come about? Material by itself cannot create laws. Who is behind their creation? And so on. These questions need to be answered and one cannot get away saying that these are working principles for explaining the processes taking place in the material world. We also hear that the laws were different at the beginning of the Universe. If so, how and why did they change with the evolution of the Universe? Further, the immaculate construction of the living species starting from single cellular amoeba to the most complex human beings having intelligence is a great mystery.

We commonly hear statements such as:

- 'I did everything possible very carefully but I did not get the result I wanted',
- 'He was an extremely disciplined and careful person with regard to his health, but he suddenly got a heart attack and died'.
- 'Life is very uncertain'
- 'Mr X and Mr Y did this work together, but only Y got the credit for it',
- 'Mr X exploits all good people to get benefits for himself',
- 'Mr X is not even half as good as me in terms of intellect and ability, but still he rises faster than me in stature',
- 'Mr Y died of an accident because of someone else's fault',
- 'A terrible train accident occurred in which 200 people died on the spot and more than 1000 have been admitted to the hospital'. The people who have died or are injured had no role to play in the accident.
- Mr X, even as a child, displayed incredible intellectual or physical or artistic abilities

which are beyond any one's imagination. Such individuals are referred to as Prodigies.

All these point to the existence of another entity which controls the Universe, and which is again abstract and beyond the reach of direct experimentation. This is super-soul referred to as Paramatma.

Spirituality starts here and deals with the abstract entities, Atma, Paramatma, Dharma, Adharma, Order etc, as well as with the material world since Atma performs all its actions on the material world.

How do we understand all the abstract entities listed above which are not accessible to direct experimental investigation? Can one think of experiments using materials only that can throw light on Atma? The answer is 'No'. The only source of information in this context is 'literature' or 'scriptures' which are fault-free, are in accordance with life experiences, and describe the relationships between the abstract entities. The scriptures which help us rationalize all such and other phenomena are called the 'Vedas' which are considered to be blemish free. These are in Sanskrit language and their validity has been established beyond doubt by many rishis, acharyas, thousands of years ago, and even today one can see several incidents validating those. We come across many incidents where some individuals have achieved feats, '*impossible even to imagine by any modern yardstick*'. These individuals seem to have acquired some powers or abilities (*siddhi*) by performing actions as prescribed in the Vedas, and by devotion to and blessings of Paramatma. We will discuss these in the next chapter.

What did Eminent Scientists say?

Who are eminent scientists? These are individuals who have achieved path-breaking research in various subjects and as such are highly respected across the communities. They are recognised by a variety of awards bestowed on them by various institutions or agencies. Among those, the so-called Nobel Prize is considered universally as the most prestigious and highly respected. This prize was created in the beginning of the 20th century, by a wealthy businessman, Alfred Nobel, who donated all his wealth for the purpose of recognising the greatest contributions by individuals in the areas of Physics, Chemistry,

Literature, Physiology & Medicine and Peace. These prizes are awarded every year after a global search without any kind of conditions with regard to nationality, race, gender, etc. The sole criterion is the uniqueness of the accomplishment and the benefit of the accomplishment to the society at large. The opinions of such personalities are highly respected world-wide.

What did such luminary personalities think about the scientific accomplishments and need or otherwise of spirituality? An exhaustive compendium of such opinions arrived at either by personal interviews or through lectures by those personalities has been published recently.

This is a book authored by Tihomir Dimitrov (copyright 1995-2008) of several hundred pages documenting the quotations of more than 100 luminaries of different times.

I will list here only a few of those opinions mostly belonging to the 20ᵗʰ century, since it is during this time that scientific developments have resulted in major technological breakthroughs.

Albert Einstein (Nobel Prize in Physics, 1921)
"Science without religion is lame and religion without science is blind"
"The more I study science, the more I believe in God"

"My religiosity consists in a humble admiration of the infinitely superior Spirit that reveals itself in the little that we, with our weak and transitory understanding, can comprehend of reality"

Max Planck (Nobel Prize in Physics, 1918)
"Both religion and science need for their activities the belief in God, and moreover, God stands for the former in the beginning, and for the latter at the end of the whole thinking"

Werner Heisenberg (Nobel Prize in Physics, 1932)
"The first gulp from the glass of natural sciences will turn you into an atheist, but at the bottom of the glass God is waiting for you"

Erwin Schrödinger (Nobel Prize in Physics, 1933)
"Consciousness cannot be accounted for in physical terms. For Consciousness is absolutely fundamental. It cannot be accounted for in terms of anything else."

Robert Millikan (Nobel Prize in Physics, 1923)
"To me it is unthinkable that a real Atheist could be a scientist. I have never known a thinking man who did not believe in God"
"It is a sublime conception of God which is furnished by science, and one wholly consonant with the highest ideals of religion, when it represents Him as revealing Himself through countless ages in the development of the earth as an abode for man and in the age-long inbreathing of life into its constituent matter, culminating in man with his spiritual nature and all his God-like powers"

"Many of our great scientists have actually been men of profound religious convictions and life: Sir Issac Newton, Michael Faraday, James Clerk Maxwell, Louis Pasteur"

Charles Townes (Nobel Prize in Physics, 1964)
"I think all of science, in a sense, comes from belief in order in the universe. That is part of scientific faith, that there is order and reliability, and so on, and that is part of Christian tradition, that there is one God"

"Life may be very improbable, but it did happen and it happened in accordance with physical laws; and physical laws are laws that God made"

Nevill Mott (Nobel Prize in Physics, 1977)
"I believe, too, that neither physical science nor psychology can ever explain human consciousness. To me, then, human consciousness lies outside science and it is here that I seek the relationship between God and man"

Derek Barton (Nobel Prize in Chemistry, 1969)
"God is Truth. There is no incompatibility between science and religion. Both are seeking the same truth. The observations and experiments of science are so wonderful that the truth that they establish can surely be accepted as another manifestation of God. God shows himself by allowing man to establish truth."

Christian Anfinsen (Nobel Prize in Chemistry, 1972)
"I think only an idiot can be an atheist. We must admit that there exists an incomprehensible power or force with limitless foresight and knowledge that started the whole Universe going, in the first place"

Sir C V Raman (Nobel Prize in Physics, 1930)
"The growing discoveries in the science of astronomy and physics seem to be further and further revelations of God."

A P J Kalam (Bharat Ratna awardee)
"God, our Creator, has stored within our minds and personalities, great potential strength and ability. Prayer helps us to tap and develop these powers."

Arthur Stanley Eddington (renowned astrophysicist)
"We have learnt that the exploration of the external world by the methods of physical science leads not to a concrete reality but to a shadow world of symbols, beneath which those methods are unadapted for penetrating. Feeling that there must be more behind, we return to our starting

point in human consciousness - the one centre where more might become known. There we find other stirrings, other revelations than those conditioned by the world of symbols... Physics most strongly insists that its methods do not penetrate behind the symbolism. Surely then that mental and spiritual nature of ourselves, known in our minds by an intimate contact transcending the methods of physics, supplies just that... which science is admittedly unable to give."

I will discuss more about the relationship between Soul, God and their importance in our daily lives in the later chapters.

Chapter 3

Prodigies and Supernatural Powers

Summary: This chapter draws attention to the fact that the world has witnessed the existence of large number of personalities who displayed incredible abilities, difficult to imagine by any logic based on modern scientific thinking. They establish a connection between science and spirituality. They establish concepts of rebirth and carrying forward of information (Sanskara or karmic account) from one birth to the next. My selection of the personalities is truly personal and certainly not exhaustive; however, it is sufficient to drive home the intended message.

PRODIGIES are individuals we have come across in this world, who displayed unimaginable abilities and strengths. The feats they accomplished cannot be logically explained by any scientific yardstick. I show below a large number of them and their feats. There are many stories which present incidents witnessed by public then, and which are beyond any comprehension, and these indicate difference between human and divine powers.

Martha Argerich

Born in 1941, pianist Martha Argerich aged 5 took up the piano, and was soon hailed as a prodigy, performing in publc

Shakuntala Devi

1929-2013 Her father discovered his daughter's ability to memorize numbers while teaching her a card trick when she was about three years old. Her father took her on road shows that displayed her ability at calculation. She did this without any formal education. At the age of six she demonstrated her arithmetic abilities at the University of Mysore.

Ramabhadracharya

The author of more than 100 books, Giridhar (born, 1950), has been blind since the age of two months, had no formal education till the age of seventeen years, and has never used Braille or any other aid to learn or compose.

- At the age of three, Giridhar composed his first piece of poetry.
- At the age of five, Giridhar memorised the entire Bhagavad Gita, consisting of around 700 verses with chapter and verse numbers, in 15 days
- At seven, he memorised the entire Ramcharitmanas of Tulsidas, consisting of around 10,900 verses with chapter and verse numbers, in 60 days
- Speaks 22 languages, author of 100 books
- Established a University for Disabled.

W. A. Mozart (1756-1791)

The young composer could pick out tunes on the piano at the age of three, and began composing by age four. By the time he was 12, he had clocked up 10 symphonies and performed for royalty.

Srinivas Ramanujan (1887-1920)

An equation means nothing to me unless it expresses a thought of God. ...

Blaise Pascal (1623-1662)

French mathematician, physicist, and religious philosopher who wrote a treatise on vibrating bodies at the age of nine; he wrote his first proof, on a wall with a piece of coal, at the age of 11 years, and a theorem by the age of 16 years.

Persons who displayed exemplary supernatural powers

Many persons through the centuries displayed exemplary supernatural powers.

Adi Shankaracharya (788-820)

Transmigration of Soul: Parakaya Pravesa: Once after giving detailed instructions to the disciples, Adi Shankaracharya abdicated his gross body, and entered the dead body of a king through his brahmarandhra, proceeding to the toe. On seeing their husband alive, unable to control their emotions, the queens screamed in joy– "Oh God! What miracle is this! What a benign merciful act by God! After a month or so, Shankaracharya returned to his own body which was preserved by his disciples on his instruction, and the King died again. With the experience he gained about 'Kamashastra' while residing in the body of the King, Shankaracharya won the debate with the wife of Mandan Mishra.

While at the Veda Patshala, Shankara as a student had to go out and beg for his food. He reached the house of a poor Brahmin woman who had nothing but half rotten gooseberries (*amalaka*). She was mentally upset that she had nothing worthwhile to give the boy to eat. Shankara wanted to save the lady from the mental agony and sang a hymn to Goddess Lakshmi which resulted in the shower of golden amalaka fruits all around the house. This hymn is known as "Kanakadara stavam".

Shankara was a prodigal child and an extraordinary scholar with almost superhuman capabilities. At the age of two, he could fluently speak and write Sanskrit. At the age of four, he could recite all the Vedas, and at the age of twelve, he took sanyas and left his home. Even at such a young age, he gathered disciples and started walking throughout the country to re-establish the spiritual sciences.

Once in a village there was a blacksmith working. Shankara went inside, picked up the pot of molten iron, drank it and walked on.

Shankara went in the search of a Guru to be formally initiated as a Sanyasi. At the banks of the river Narmada, he found the river gushing forth and the flood waters were about to enter the cave of his Guru. By using his powers, he encapsulated the flood waters in his Kamandal (a vessel sannyasi's carry) and released it in the banks of the river. Sri Govinda Bagawathpada, an ascetic who saw this, marvelled at Sri Shankara and took him on as a Shishya.

Once, in Kasi, when Sri Shankara was going to the Vishwanath Temple, his path was blocked by an "untouchable" who was accompanied by his wife and 4 dogs. The disciples of Sri Shankara shouted at him to make way, and to keep a distance. The untouchable smiled and said, "According to your principle of Advaita, which you practice, all the Jivatma are same as God. How do you ask me to go? How am I different from your Paramacharya? What you say is unreasonable. How can I go away from myself?" Sri Shankara realised that it was not an ordinary person and understood that it was Lord Shiva himself who had come along with His consort and the four Vedas. He prostrated before the Lord and sang five slokas called "Manisha Panchakam". Lord Shiva presented himself along with Visalakshi and blessed Sri Shankara.

Shankara changed the course of river Purna to bring it closer to his house for his aged mother: One day Shankara›s aged mother who was weak due to fasts and other ascetic observances, fell down exhausted when she went to take her bath in the *river Purna*, which was at some distance from the house. Shankara worried by his mother's condition invoked the river deity to turn her course nearer his home. The river deity, pleased with the invocation of Shankara turned the course of the river through the neighbourhood of Shankara's home.

Sri Ramanujacharya (1017-1137)

During the last rites of Alavandar, a Guru of Ramanuja, people noticed that three fingers of Alavandar remained folded signifying three of his last unfulfilled wishes. As Ilaya Perumal (Ramanuja) swore (i) that he would write a commentary on Vedavyasa's Brahma Sutra (ii) that he would perpetuate the memory of Vyasa and Parasara and (iii) that he would strive to propagate Visishtadvaita the fingers unfolded one by one automatically and stretched out to normal position.

Once, Sri Ramanuja went to a sacred place in Tamil Nadu, namely, "Tiru Narayana Puram" to collect white clay paste used for applying Tilak (religious mark). The deity of the temple there had been taken away by the Muslim invaders and was being used as a doll by the muslim princess in Delhi to play among themselves. Ramanuja went to Delhi and lovingly called 'Come on! My dear child". The idol miraculously came onto his lap. Then, Ramanuja reinstalled it in the temple.

Once, fearing that one day, Sri Ramanuja would demolish Advaita philosophy, the advaitin pandit Yadava Prakasa plotted to kill Sri Ramanuaja while on a pilgrimage tour of the country with his disciples. Knowing this plan through his relative Govindan, Sri Ramanuaja slipped out into the forest at dead of night. Miraculously, an aged hunter couple appeared and guided him. They rested for the night and next day morning Ramanuja found himself at the outskirts of Kanchipuram, his home town, and the couple had disappeared. He realized that it was Lord Varadaraja and Perundevi Mother who had come in the guise of the hunter couple.

Sri Madhwacharya (1238-1317)

Once, when he was only 3-4 years old (his name then was Vasudeva), he was asked by his mother to protect the curds and milk kept in the pots from cats. Being playful and restive child, he lifted two huge pieces of granites and closed the milk and curd pots. These mosuru kallu (curd stone) and Halu kallu (milk stone) has been preserved for the posterity, even today at Pajaka kshetra.

Once Acharya was travelling through the Goa region. A Brahmana named Shankara invited him to his place. He wanted to test him, so he offered 4000 banana fruits to him which was first offered to God. Acharya ate all of them and later drank 30 vessels full of milk.

At Ambuthertha where river Bhadra flows, a huge block of stone—length of this stone is 6.1 meters, breadth 3.6 meters and height

10.98 meters (~50 tons) – which a number of people together found impossible to move, Madhwacharya lifted with one hand and placed it in the proper place effortlessly. An inscription in Sanskrit, stating this, can be found on the stone even today.

Sri Madhwacharya exhibited many more supernatural actions during his lifetime which are briefly listed below.

o   Fasting for 48 days.

o   As a child he killed a big serpent by crushing its head under his toe, near his home town

o   Walking on the river Ganges, garments not getting wet

o   Talking to a Muslim King in Persian

o   Saving disciples from thieves in a magical way; they all appeared like rocks when the thieves approached them.

o   Wrestling; mighty wrestlers could not squeeze his neck or even move his one toe.

o   Making a seed grow into a plant by reciting Vedas, when the validity of Vedas was challenged.

o   On the day of an eclipse, when he was going to the ocean for a bath, he stopped the huge waves and made the ocean look like a lake.

o When Satyateertha, one of his disciples tried to follow him to Badrinath through a hilly route and could not keep pace with him, he translocated Satyateertha to his ashram on the ground by the wave of his one hand.

o Using his *danda* (stick) to strike the earth and produce water to quench the thirst of a pregnant lady. This place is now a pilgrimage site called DandaTeertha

o On Malpe beach, saved a drowning ship by using his power to move matter from a long distance. The softstone block gifted by the ship's captain at the request of the Acharya had the idols of Krishna and Balaram. Acharya installed the Krishna idol in Udupi Temple.

o His disciple, Sri Trivikrama Panditacharya once peeked in while Sri Madhwacharya was worshipping Lord Vishnu. He could see:
Sri Hanuman worshipping Sri Ram.
Sri Bhimasena worshipping Sri Krishna.
Sri Madhwacharya worshipping Sri Vedavyasa (Avatar of Vishnu).

o He possessed out of the world knowledge. He never studied anything during Gurukul life.

o He would mesmerize his Gurus and people

by reciting lessons that were not even taught to him by them in any class.

He did not die. He vanished out of thin air. When he was teaching his disciples the Upanishads in Udupi, there was a shower of flowers from the skies, and when the flowers were cleared, he was not to be seen. It is believed that Madhwacharya is still residing in Badrinath with maharshi Vedavyasa.

Sri Jayateertha (1345-1388) also known as Sri Tikacharya

Jayateertha (Dondopant before talking Sanyas) is considered to be incarnation of Indra with an Avesha of Adi-Shesha. When his father got him married at the age of 20 against his wish to prevent him from taking sanyas, he showed his form as a big snake in the bedroom. Then his father realized that Dondopant was no ordinary person and allowed him to take sanyas, and then he became Jayateertha. He displayed exemplary knowledge, sharpness in debates, and skills, and wrote commentaries on all the works of Madhwacharya – which were very brief and crisp

- and authored independent granthas as well, all of which laid down the foundation for proper interpretation of the scriptures. These have become indispensable to understand Madhwa philosophy. Therefore, he became popular as Tikacharya.

Sri Raghavendra Teertha (1595 – 1671)

Sri Raghavendra Teertha, also called Rayaru, displayed exemplary supernatural powers during his lifetime. A few are listed below.

Once a king offered a jewelled necklace to Swamiji and the same was put by Swamiji in the Fire of Sacrifice. The king felt insulted. The Swamiji knew his (King's) disturbances in mind and prayed to ParasuRama, the in-dweller of Fire God, and showed his amazing powers by getting it back. The king realized that Raghavendra Swamy possessed divine powers.

Nawab of Adoni, Sidhi Masud Khan, tested the prowess of Raghavendra Swamy by placing a plate containing meat before the seer. Rayaru accepted the offering and sprinkled holy water from his kamandala. When the clothe covering the plate was removed, the meat had turned into fruits and flowers.

Sir Thomas Munroe was asked to resume Mantralaya an endowment village granted to maintain the Mutt and temple at Mantralaya. When he came Sri Rayaru emerged from the Brindavan and convinced him about the irrevocability of the endowment and disappeared into the Brindavan giving him 'Mantrakshate'. Sri Rayaru was visible to Mr. Munroe only and not to others. This episode is recorded in the Madras Gazettier in the First quarter of 19th Century, copy of which can be pursued even today in the records at the Collectorate at Anantapur.

Once when Rayaru was travelling, an atheist headman who did not believe in God, mantras or Vedas challenged him to a confrontation and asked him to prove the efficacy of the Veda mantras. He produced a dry and hard piece of dead wood and asked Rayaru to make it sprout leaves. Rayaru chanted Veda mantras and sprinkled water from his kamandala on it. Within a short time, the wood sprouted fresh green leaves, vindicating Rayaru's words.

EXTRACT FROM

"MADRAS DISTRICT GAZETTEERS"

By **W. FRANCIS**, Esq, I.C.S

VOLUME NO. 1, BELLARY.

Reprint 1916 by the Superintendent Govt. Press, Madras

Chapter XV--- Adoni Taluk -Page No.213

Mantsala (Mantralaya):- A Shrotriem village with a population of 1212 on the bank of the Tungabhadra in the extreme north of the taluk. The village is widely known as containing the tomb of the Madhva saint Sri Raghavendra Swami, the annual festival in August connected with, which is attended by large numbers of pilgrims, including even Lingayats, from Bombay, the Nizam's Dominions and even Mysore. The tomb itself is not of architectural interest. The grant of the landed endowment attached to it, is said in one of the Mackenzie MSS, to have been made by Venkanna Pant, the well known Dewan of Sidi Masaud Khan, Governor of Adoni from 1662 to 1687.

A quaint story of Sir Thomas Munro is told about the place. The endowment being threatened with resumption, Munro, it is said, came to make enquiries. After removing his boots and taking off his hat he approached the grave. The saint thereupon emerged from his tomb and met him. They conversed together for some time regarding the resumption, but though the saint was visible and audible to Munro - who was himself the people declare, semi-divine, none of the others who were there could either see him or hear what he said. The discussion ended, Munro returned to his tent and quashed the proposal to resme the endowment. Being offered some concentrated rice, he accepted it and ordered it to be used in the preparation of his meals for that day.

-Madras Review vii 280

Sri Vijayeendra Teertha (1517-1614)

Sri Vijayeendra Teertha was the exponent of 64 types of skills mentioned in the scriptures. He defeated a large number of experts who came to challenge him on different skills. While doing so he displayed incredible supernatural powers. I will list here a few of those.

Once, news spread that Delhi Sultan's army was nearing the temple town of Kumbakonam. People & devotees were more worried about the temples. They immediately contacted Sri Vijayendra Teertha swamigal & requested him to save Kumbakonam. He is not the king or maintaining army. There was a small army of

Maratha King guarding Kombakonam. News was sent to the king in Tanjore for reinforcement. But they could not reach in time. Now, people felt that swamigal only could save them & Kumbakonam. Swamigal assured them that they need not worry. It was evening time. He prayed & distributed 5000 coconuts in the mutt to the people. He instructed them to break them in the entrance & around the temple when the invaders attack the temple. People remained awake throughout the night. In the morning, the army of Delhi sultan reached Kumbakonam & began attacking the temples. Devotees started breaking coconuts. Invaders fell down from their horses one by one & every time they heard the sound of breaking of coconuts, they felt unbearable head ache in their heads & felt that an unknown power was preventing them from attacking. Immediately, they left Kumbakonam fearing for their lives.

Lingarajendra, a famous shaiva saint came to know that Sri Vijayeendra Teertha was a great Madhwa philosopher. He could not tolerate the fame, reputation Vijayeendra Teertha had achieved. He invited Swamiji for a debate, and Kumbeshwara temple at Kumbakonam was fixed as the venue. Swamiji started from his mutt to

Kumbheshwar temple in a pallakki (palanquin) and the shaiva sanyasi also started the same way from his mutt. They both met at one road corner. Now the shaiva sanyasi got down from his palanquin and told his shishyas to place the vyagraasana (tiger skin) on the wall of a compound of a house. The wall started moving towards the temple. Then, Sri Vijayeendra Teertha asked his shisyaas to take off their hands from the palanquin. Now, the palaquin along with the Swamiji itself moved high in the sky and landed in front of the Kumbheswara temple.

Sri Kanaka Dasa (1509-1609)

There are many popular legends regarding Lord Krishna's revelation to Kanakadasa. The most popular legend is that Kanakadasa came to Udupi as a pilgrim to visit the temple. Sri Vadiraja Tirtha had heard about this pious devotee of the Lord and made arrangements for his stay in a hut on the roadside in front of the temple. Kanaka Dâsa used to play on his tambura and sing in the hut, but he used to think of how the idol of Krishna looked like. Being of a lower caste, by tradition he was forbidden to enter the temple and have darshana of Krishna. The wall of the shrine was in between the idol and Kanakadasa

When Kanakadasa secretly entered the temple, he was caught by the temple authorities without Vadiraja's knowledge. He was whipped and chained as a punishment, in front of the back wall of the sanctum. In desperate pain, he sang a song *Baagilanu teredu, Seveyanu kodo Hariye* (Open the door, O Hari and give me the opportunity to serve you), When he finished singing, his chains snapped, an earthquake occurred and the wall exploded, shattering the bricks. The idol, which was traditionally facing the east, miraculously turned towards the west in front of Kanakadasa's face. Kanakadasa had the darshana of Krishna. Vadiraja got to know of the crack and instead of having the crack plastered over, he enlarged it and turned it into a window, knowing that once the idol has turned, it will never return to its original position. In memory of Kanakadasa, the window is named *Kanakana Kindi* (Kanaka›s window)

According to Agama Shastras, Hindu temples and their idols are to be built, facing the east, since the east is considered auspicious as the Sun rises from the east. The Udupi Krishna temple is an exception, visitors enter from the East and go around to see the idol which faces West. A window with nine viewing apertures exists where the wall cracked and the idol is visible from the window. Due to Kanakadasa's incident, everyone, irrespective of their caste is allowed into the temple. A tradition goes that only after looking at the idol, the visitors and temple priests will enter the temple.

One can list many more such prodigies and personalities with supernatural powers, but it is not the intention here to be exhaustive. Rather, I wish to drive the point that the occurrence of prodigies on this planet testifies to the existence of God, from whom they acquired supernatural powers and abilities by his grace.

Chapter 4

The Ancient Indian Wisdom

Summary: This chapter aims at bringing to the fore the wisdom and knowledge which our ancestors had thousands of years ago, with regard to science and technology, on one hand, and spirituality (consciousness and its relation to the world) on the other, so that together with modern science it can help mankind in enhancing the quality of life. I cover here only a small portion of the vast and enormous ancient wisdom, as illustration, and consequently, I focus only on topics covered in the previous chapters; firstly, on concepts with regard to evolution of the universe and, then, largely on health-related issues which are crucial for leading a healthy life. Even here, I provide only a glimpse into the vast field, just to be motivational for the common people. Interestingly, many of the ancient concepts are in resonance with the modern thoughts which have been arrived at by extensive experimentation.

WHAT is the kind of wisdom our ancestors had? Here we can consider history of several thousands of years. How did they live their lives? Is there anything one can learn from them which can improve the quality of life today? What was the source of their knowledge? And so on. I will limit my discussion here to only that which relates to India alone, and, I believe, similar discussion should possibly apply to other parts of the world as well.

What scholars and historians of today do agree is that the source of knowledge that drove all activities in the ancient times was the so-called 'Vedas'. Ramayana and Mahabharat are two other commonly accepted authentic scriptures and sources of information – these two were authored by Maharshi Valmiki and Maharshi Vedavyas respectively. This word 'Vedas' itself has origin in the Sanskrit language and means, 'that which gives knowledge'. Vedas are considered to be self-evident and 'apourusheya, meaning not composed by any individual', hence blemish-free, and therefore, their contents represent the ultimate truth. God is the only person who has complete knowledge of these Vedas. On this count some philosophers argued that He might have created the Vedas. However, Lord Krishna who is the incarnation of God himself, declared in Bhagvadgita that he did not compose Vedas but only knew them. Since God is eternal, the Vedas are also eternal. Maharshi Vedavyasa, who is also considered to be the incarnation of God himself grouped them into four parts which were called as 'Rigveda', 'Yajurveda', 'Samaveda' and 'Atharvaveda'. Each of these was further sub-divided according to their content into,

- Aranyakas (Forest texts)– Philosophical interpretations of vedic rituals
- Brahmanas – explanations and instructions on vedic rituals
- Samhitas – hymns, prayers, mantras in vedic rituals
- Upanishads – philosophical knowledge

The Vedas are also called as 'Shruti' since these were learnt through ages, only by listening to oral transmission from Gurus (teachers) to Shishyas (students), the first Guru being God himself. Notwithstanding the eternal nature of the Vedas, maharshi Vedavyasa presented them about 8-10 thousand years ago (these numbers are debatable) to the mankind. The information in the Vedas is presented in the Sanskrit language. Therefore, much of my quotes here will be in the Sanskrit language, but at most places English translations are also included.

Maharshi Vedavyasa has also narrated, as stories in simple language, historical incidents to explain the purport of the Vedas. These works are known as Puranas. These are eighteen in number namely, Matsya, Markandeya, Varaha, Bhavishya, Bhagavata, Brahma, Brahma Vaivarta, Brahmananda, Vamana, Kurma, Vishnu, Agni, Naradiya, Padma, Shiva, linga, Garuda and Skanda. All the activities of the people were driven strictly according to the prescriptions in these 'scriptures'. Vedavyasa also wrote the so-called Brahmasutras which constitute the greatest aids for interpreting the Vedas. An important component of Mahabharata is the 'Bhagvadgita' which is supposed to be the summary of all Upanishads in imparting knowledge.

सर्वोपनिषदो गावो दोग्धा गोपालनन्दनः।
पार्थो वत्सः सुधीर्भोक्ता दुग्धं गीतामृतं महत्॥४॥

Meaning: If the entire Upanishads are likened to cows, the milker is the son of the cowherd, Gopalanandana and Arjuna (partha) is the calf. The men of purified intellect are the drinkers and the milk is the supreme nectar of Gita.

Many Acharyas wrote commentaries (Bhashyas) on the Vedas, the Bhagavadgita and the Puranas, interpreting them as supporting their philosophies. The Vedas contain information about all things that are knowable?, and some of these aspects are summarised below.

Creation

1. Paramatma (God) is the Creator of this universe. He is referred to as 'Anant Koti Brahmanda Nayak'. These refer to infinite types of universes. He has created these effortlessly, as a sport and without any outside help, by his own wish and energy in a systematic manner. In the scriptures, Paramatma is known by various names (in

fact they are infinite). The most common ones are: 'Narayana', 'Vasudeva', 'Keshava', 'Krishna', 'Vishnu', 'Brahma', 'Narasimha', 'Rama', to list some. Some of the various scriptural evidences for the statements describing creation are given below.

A. Bhagavadita
Lord Krishna who is God himself says the following in Bhagavadgita.

अहं सर्वस्य प्रभवो मत्त: सर्व प्रवर्तते |
इति मत्वा भजन्ते मां बुधा भावसमन्विता: ||८||

BG 10.8: I am the origin of all creation. Everything proceeds from Me. The wise who know this perfectly worship Me with great faith and devotion.

B. Bhagavat Puran SB 2.10.12
Maharshi Vedavyas who is the incarnation of God says the following in Bhagavat Puran.

द्रव्यं कर्म च कालश्च स्वभावो जीव एव च ।
यदनुग्रहत: सन्ति न सन्ति यदुपेक्षया ||१२||

Meaning: One should definitely know that all

material ingredients, activities, time and modes, and the living entities who are meant to enjoy them all, exist by His mercy only, and as soon as He does not care for them, everything becomes nonexistent.

Bhagavat Puran SB 6.16.37

क्षित्यादिभिरेष किलावृत: सप्तभिर्दशगुणोत्तरैरण्डकोश: ।
यत्र पतत्यणुकल्प: सहाण्डकोटिकोटिभिस्तदनन्त: ॥३७॥

Meaning: Every universe is covered by seven layers— earth, water, fire, air, sky, the total energy and false ego—each ten times greater than the previous one. There are innumerable universes besides this one, and although they are unlimitedly large, they move about like atoms in You. Therefore, You are called unlimited [ananta].

Bhagavat Puran SB 10.87.41

द्युपतय एव ते न ययुरन्तमनन्ततयात्वमपि
यदन्तराण्डनिचया ननु सावरणा: ।
ख इव रजांसि वान्ति वयसा सह यच्छ्रुतय-स्त्वयि हि
फलन्त्यतन्निरसनेन भवन्निधना: ॥४१॥

Meaning: Because You are unlimited, neither the lords of heaven nor even You Yourself can ever reach the end of Your glories. The countless universes, each enveloped in its shell, are compelled by the wheel of time to wander within You, like particles of dust blowing about in the sky. The śrutis, following their method of eliminating everything separate from the Supreme, become successful by revealing You as their final conclusion.

Bhagavat Puran SB 3.11.41

दशोत्तराधिकैर्यत्र प्रविष्टः परमाणुवत् ।
लक्ष्यतेऽन्तर्गताश्चान्ये कोटिशो ह्याण्डराशयः ॥४१॥

Meaning: The layers or elements covering the universes are each ten times thicker than the one before, and all the universes clustered together appear like atoms in a huge combination.

C. Nasidiya Sukta (Rig Veda)

नासदासीन्नो सदासीत्तदानीं नासीद्रजो नो व्योमा परो यत् ।
किमावरीवः कुह कस्य शर्मन्नम्भः किमासीद्गहनं गभीरम् ॥१॥

Meaning: Then even non-existence was not there, nor existence, There was no air then, nor the space beyond it. What covered it? Where was it? In whose keeping? Was there then cosmic fluid, in depths unfathomed?

न मृत्युरासीदमृतं न तर्हि न रात्र्या अह्न आसीत्प्रकेतः ।
आनीदवातं स्वधया तदेकं तस्माद्धान्यन्न परः किञ्चनास ॥२॥

Meaning: Then there was neither death nor immortality nor was there then the torch of night and day. The One breathed windlessly and self-sustaining. There was that One then, and there was no other.

तम आसीत्तमसा गूहळमग्रे प्रकेतं सलिलं सर्वाऽइदम् |
तुच्छ्येनाभ्वपिहितं दासीत्तपसस्तन्महिनाजायतैकम् ॥३॥

Meaning: At first there was only darkness wrapped in darkness. All this was only unillumined cosmic water. That One which came to be, enclosed in nothing, arose at last, born of the power of knowledge.

कामस्तदग्रे समवर्तताधि मनसो रेतः प्रथमं यदासीत् |
सतो बन्धुमसति निरविन्दन्हृदि प्रतीष्या कवयो मनीषा ॥४॥

Meaning: In the beginning desire descended on it - that was the primal seed, born of the mind. The sages who have searched their hearts with wisdom know that which is, is kin to that which is not.

तिरश्चीनो विततो रश्मिरेषामधः स्विदासीदुपरि स्विदासीत् |
रेतोधा आसन्महिमान आसन्त्स्वधा अवस्तात्प्रयतिः परस्तात् ॥५॥

Meaning: And they have stretched their cord across the void, and know what was above, and what below. Seminal powers made fertile mighty forces.

Below was strength, and over it was impulse.

को अद्धा वेद क इह प्र वोचत्कुत आजाता कुत इयं विसृष्टिः |
अर्वाग्देवा अस्य विसर्जनेनाथा को वेद यत आबभूव ॥६॥

Meaning: But, after all, who knows, and who can say Whence it all came, and how creation happened? the gods themselves are later than creation, so who knows truly whence it has arisen?

इयं विसृष्टिर्यत आबभूव यदि वा दधे यदि वा न |
यो अस्याध्यक्षः परमे व्योमन्त्सो अङ्ग वेद यदि वा न वेद ॥७॥

Meaning: Whence all creation had its origin, the creator, whether he fashioned it or whether he did not, the creator, who surveys it all from highest heaven,he knows — or maybe even he does not know.

D. Brahmasutras

ॐ जन्माद्यस्य यतः ॐ ॥ 02-02 ॥

सृष्टिस्थितिसंहारनियमनज्ञानाज्ञानबन्धमोक्षा यतः ।

This is the Brahmasutra of Vedavyasa which uniquely characterises Paramatma as the one responsible for: Creation (Srishti), Maintenance (Stithi), Destruction (Laya), Knowledge (Jnyana), Ignorance (Ajnyana), Bandhana (engaging the souls in the cycle of births and deaths), Liberation of the Souls (Moksha) and finally, Control (Niyamana) of everything. Brahmasutras were created to convey the purport of the Vedas (there are a total of 564 sutras organized in Four chapters).

2. Explosion of a Brahmanda (golden egg or cosmic egg) marks the beginning of a universe, and in each universe, creation and destruction happen every day (referred to as Kalpa) of Brahma – one day of Brahma is 8.64 billion earth years. Brahma's life span, is hundred years – each year is 360 days. Interestingly, modern theories are also contemplating on multiple universes.

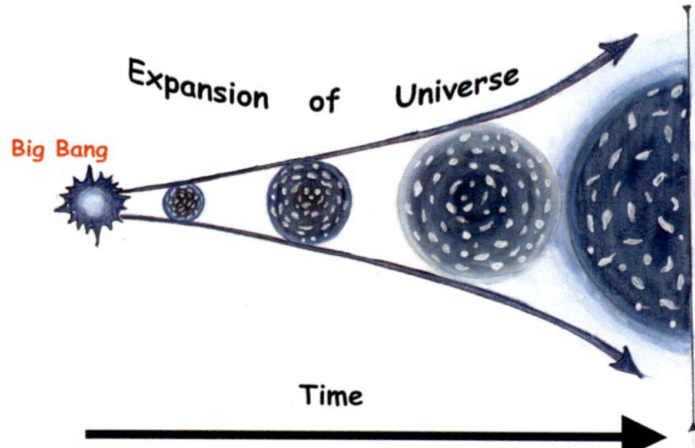

Drawing from the above scriptures and many more, the systematic process of creation in each universe is described in the following slokas of Manimanjari composed by Sri Narayana Panditacharya in the 13th century.

Manimanjari

ससर्ज भगवानदौ त्रीन्गुणान् प्रकृतेः परः ।
महतत्वं ततो विष्णुः सृष्टवान् ब्रह्मणस्तनुम् ॥२॥

महत्तत्वादहङ्कारं ससर्ज शिवविग्रहम् ।
दैवन्देहान्मनः खानि खं च स त्रिविधात्ततः ॥३॥

आकाशादसृजद्वायुं वायोस्तेजो व्यजीजनत् ।
तेजसः सलिलं तस्मात् पृथिवीमसृजद्द्विभुः ॥४॥

Meaning(2): First, Bhagavan created three gunas (Sattva, Rajas, Tamas) from Jada prakriti (#). From them, Bhagavan Vishnu created Mahatattva, which is the body (@) of Virinchi (Chaturmukha Brahma).

Notes
 # 'Jada Prakriti' or 'Moola prakriti' (Material cause of the world) is not created in the true sense. It is beginingless and endless (anaadi nitya).
@ Body of Virinchi means, the Mahatattva is patronised by him. Virinchi is the Patron deity for 'Mahatattva' (Abhimani Devata).

Meaning (3): From Mahatattva, Bhagavan Narayana created Ahamkara tattva, the body of Siva (ie. Siva is the patron deity for Ahamkara Tattva). From this three – fold ahamkara tattva, He created the bodies of all deities (Devatas), Mind (Manas), Sense organs (Indriyas) and Space (Bhutakasha).

Meaning(4): omnipotent Narayana created air (Vayu) from space, heat from air, water (Salila) from heat (Tejas), Earth (mud or clay) from water.

Some correlations can be made between the process of evolution as described in the scriptures with our current understanding of the same from modern science. For example, the earliest step in the process of creation by the God (referred to as Bhagavan), is the creation of the three gunas *(Sattva, Rajas, Tamas)* which represent material, and they can be likened to the most fundamental particles of modern science, namely, 'quarks' which are the integral elements of the stable elementary particles, electron, proton, neutron etc, which were created at the earliest phase of the Universe. The scriptures describe the next step of evolution as creation of the deities who were empowered by the God to create various other material objects in the universe, namely, stars, galaxies, planets, air, water, earth (heavy elements), fire etc. The bodies of the various living species were created by 'Chaturmukha Brahma'.

In this vein, one can also see that Rig Veda talks about the distances between the Sun, the Moon and the Earth which are amazingly close to the current scientific estimates. What technology did our ancestors have?

Modern science estimates (in miles) are:
Diameters: Moon – 2,171; Earth –
7,964; Sun – 8,70,438
Distances: Moon-Earth : 2,38,900;
Earth – Sun : 93.64 m

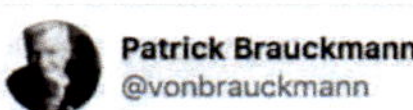

Patrick Brauckmann
@vonbrauckmann

Rig Veda is considered the oldest known text on the planet at pre 10,000 BC. It reminds us that the Dharmic culture of India knew the average distance from the Earth to both Moon and Sun were 108 times their diameters. How extraordinary and yet mysterious culture. 108.

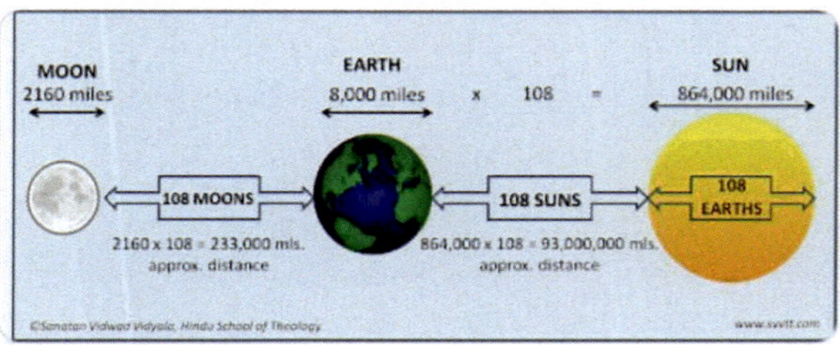

Paramatma is the one, and the only one, supreme commander, Sarvatantra - Swatantra, all powerful, all pervasive, eternal, and knowing everything about everything (Sarvajnya). He is the Sustainer and the Destroyer too. Creation and destruction of the Universes happen repeatedly. It is said that Universe is also eternal but undergoes transformation (vikara) at His will. Therefore, creation and destruction are identified with ejection from (creation) or absorption within (destruction) Paramatma Himself of the Universe and the souls. He is responsible for the Order in the Universe, controls the Universe and also the souls in every life.

Among the various vedas, Atharva Veda and its subsidiary (upaveda) Ayurveda are the most relevant in the context of science, technology, administration, healthcare etc. In this regard, the contents of Atharva Veda as described by Acharya Baldev Prasad Upadhyay are summarily listed below.

Bhaisajya Sukta –	Treatments for diseases and medicines
Ayushya Sukta –	Prayers for long life
Poushtik Sukta –	Building Houses and Agriculture

Prayashit Sukta –   Repentence for wrong acts and remedies

Streekarma Sukta – Marriage and love related issues

Rajkarma Sukta –   Kings and their duties and Responsibilities

As can be seen the various 'Suktas' describe matters related to (i) health care (ii) long life (iii) agriculture and food (iv) forbidden actions and corrective measures (v) marriage related matters and (vi) administration and governance. In the following, I will briefly present aspects related to health care as described in Ayurveda which is a branch of Atharva Veda.

Ayurvedic Biology and Health Care

The entire cosmos is viewed as an interplay of the energies of the five great elements—Space, Air, Fire, Water and Earth (mud or clay). These are called as 'panchamahabhutas'. Vata, Pitta and Kapha are combinations and permutations of these five elements that manifest as patterns present in all creation.

[सर्व द्रव्यं पाञ्चभौतिकम् । (च. सू. २६/१०)]

Ayurvedic Biology deals with the systematic evolution of the universe and life as shown in the following cartoon diagram.

The Vedas mention, there are 8.4 million types of living species, and in each type, there are innumerable number of objects (souls), which generally undergo multiple births and deaths. Further, each soul is intrinsically different from the other partly because of the different amount

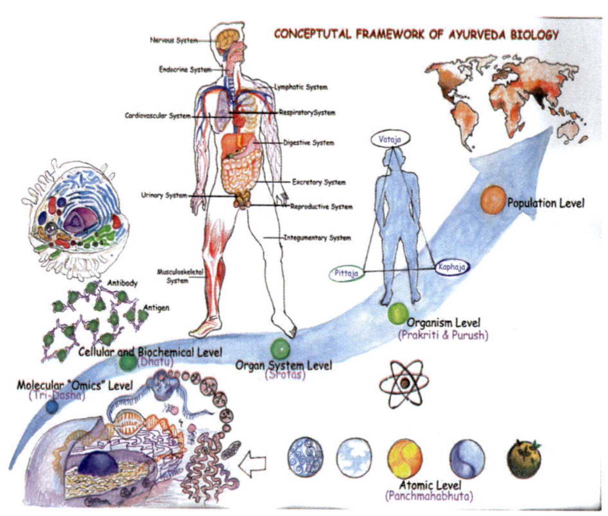

and quality of Sanskar (also referred to as Karmic Account) from the previous births. Accordingly, their bodies will have different characteristics in terms of strengths, physical features, intellect, personality etc. This gets reflected in their behaviors and actions.

Modern science puts the figure at 8.7 million (plus or minus 1.3 million) with regard to the number of types of species. The uncertainty in the modern science figure arises mainly from the way the categorization is made. The Vedic figure is incredibly close to the scientific estimate.

While treating diseases, Ayurveda focuses on the Inner balance of the Body (Prakriti) Constitution, which is determined at the time of conception and remains the same throughout one's life. The constitution is defined in terms of three basic entities: vata, pitta and kapha, also known as doshas.

Vata – composed of Space and Air. Controls movement

Pitta – made up of Fire and Water. Controls transformation

Kapha – formed from Earth and Water — and provides the "glue" that holds the cells together.

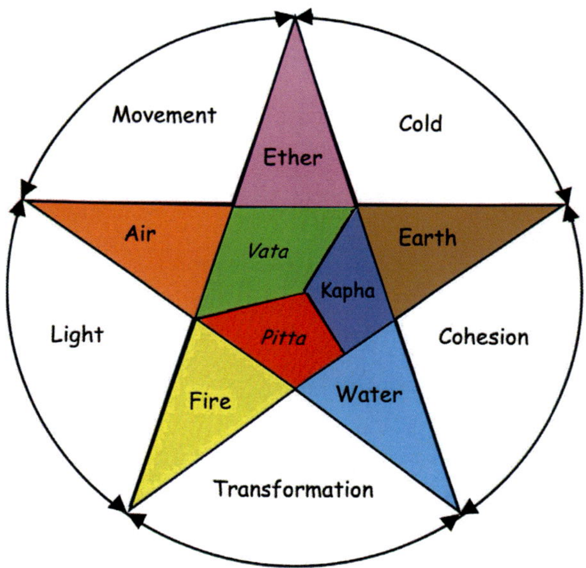

Body, mind and consciousness work together in maintaining balance of the three doshas.

Ayurveda maintains that all life must be supported by the above energies in balance. When there is minimal stress and the flow of energy through the Nadis and Chakras within a person is balanced, the body's natural defence systems will be strong and can more easily defend against disease. The following image indicates the energy centres (Chakras) and the channels (Nadis) for flow of energy through the body.

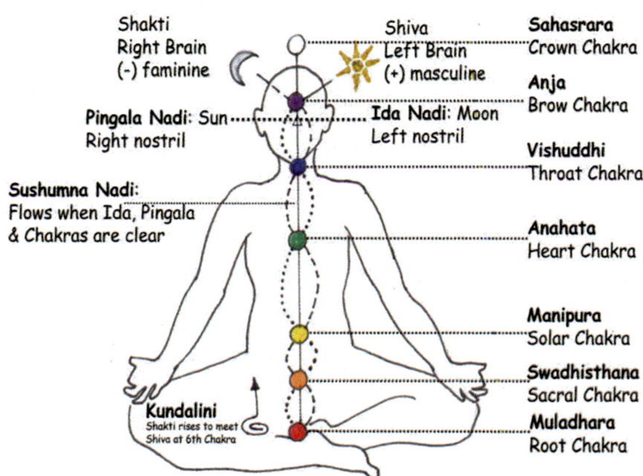

The 3 Major Nadis (rivers) and the 7 Chakras (wheels of energy)

When our emotions are out of balance, these Chakras and Nadis become blocked which manifest as illness, aches or pains in the body.

Yoga and Meditation

Meditation is recommended for all *Prakritis,* it helps in controlling the Mind. Yoga is briefly defined as follows:

Lord Krishna defines yoga in Bhagavadgita as **"Samatvam Yoga Uchyate"** (Yoga is defined as balanced state). Maharshi Patanjali defines it as, **"Chitta, Vritti, Nirodaha"** (control of mind and actions). Both indicate the following.

Yoga for clearing blocked Chakras   Meditation

Yoga is a Healer – can balance the Doshas. There are *Prakriti* specific Asanas

- Yoga is a balanced state of the body and mind.
- Yoga is a balanced state of emotions.
- Yoga is a balanced state of thoughts and intellect.
- Yoga is a balanced state of behaviour. We are excited in the situation of pleasure and we become sad when it is a negative situation.
- Yoga is to maintain equilibrium of the mind in any situation. This equanimity of mind is the ultimate objective of yoga.

सुखदु:खे समे कृत्वा लाभालाभौ जयाजयौ |

BG 2.38: Treating alike happiness and distress, loss and gain, victory and defeat.

Ashtanga Yoga

युक्ताहारविहारस्य युक्तचेष्टस्य कर्मसु |
युक्तस्वप्नावबोधस्य योगो भवति दुःखहा ||१७||

BG 6.17: *Those who are temperate in eating and recreation, balanced in work, and regulated in sleep, can mitigate all sorrows by practicing Yog.*

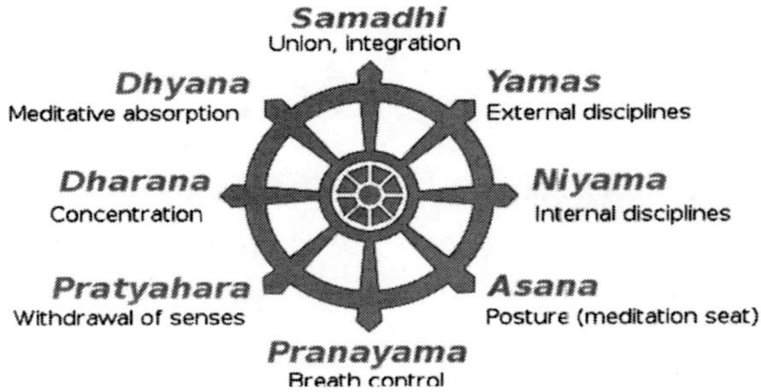

DHYANA
MEDITATION IN YOGA

तत्रैकाग्रं मनः कृत्वा यतचित्तेन्द्रियक्रियः ।
उपविश्यासने युञ्ज्याद्योगमात्मविशुद्धये ।।१२।।
समं कायशिरोग्रीवं धारयन्नचलं स्थिरः ।
संप्रेक्ष्य नासिकाग्रं स्वं दिशश्चानवलोकयन् ।।१३।।

BG 6.12-13: Seated firmly, the yogi should strive to purify the mind by focusing it in meditation with one-pointed concentration, controlling all thoughts and activities. He must hold the body, neck, and head firmly in a straight line, and gaze at the tip of the nose, without allowing the eyes to wander.

Diet, Diseases and Herbal Medicine

The most authentic modern texts describing ayurvedic knowledge regarding medicines, surgery in the ancient times are: Charak Samhita, Shushruta Samhita and Ashtangahradayam.

Sushruta Samhita describes more than 500 surgeries. Charak Samhita gives account of diseases, their treatments using herbs, and Ashtanga Hradayam is devoted to yoga, meditation etc. These are today standard texts for all the practitioners of ayurvedic medicine.

According to Ayurveda diseases occur as a result of imbalance of the three doshas: vata, pitta and kapha. (Ashtang Hriday Sutrasthanam, Chapter 11)

Symptoms of increased Pitta

पित्तम् : पीतविण्मूत्रनेत्रत्वक्क्षुत्तृड्दाहाल्पनिद्रताः

1. yellow discoloration of the faeces, urine, eyes, and skin;
2. excess of hunger and thirst,
3. feeling of burning sensation and
4. very little sleep.

Symptoms of increased Vata

कार्श्यकाष्ण्यंउष्णकामित्वकम्पानाहशकृत्ग्रहान्
बलनिद्रेन्द्रियभ्रंशप्रलापभ्रमदीनताः

1. karshya – emaciation,
2. karshnya – black discoloration,
3. ushnakamitva – desire for hot things,
4. kampa – tremors
5. anaha – bloating, fullness, distention of the

abdomen,

6. shakrut graha – constipation,

7. bala bhramsha – loss of strength,

8. nidra bhramsha – loss of sleep

9. indriya bhramsha – loss of sensory functions,

10. pralapa – irrelevant speech,

11. bhrama – delusion, dizziness giddiness

12. deenata – timidity, peevishness

Symptoms of increased of Kapha

श्लेष्मा अग्निसदनप्रसेकालस्यगौरवम्
श्वैत्यशैत्यशलथाङ्गत्वं श्वासकासातिनिद्रताः

1. agnisadana – weak digestive activity,

2. praseka – excess salivation,

3. alasya – lassitude, laziness

4. gaurava – feeling of heaviness,

5. shvaithya – white discoloration,

6. shaithya – coldness,

7. shlathangatva – looseness of the body parts,

8. shwasa – dyspnoea, asthma

9. kasa – cough, cold

10. atinidrata – excess of sleep.

Symptoms due to decrease in the doshas have also been described in the ayurvedic texts. The treatment aims at establishing the balance of the doshas in the whole system rather than on reducing the symptoms. This is a feature which distinguishes ayurveda from modern medicine which is often referred to as 'allopathy'. Moreover, since ayurveda aims at the whole body, whose composition (prakriti) is different for different individuals, the treatment essentially becomes person centric.

This is often termed as 'personalised medicine', or in a layman language, 'one dress does not fit all'. It is interesting to know that at the current times, allopathy is also envisaging such a concept. While allopathy helps remove painful symptoms rather quickly and hence reduces suffering, and ayurveda provides a long - lasting cure, a combination of the two approaches is suggested to be more beneficial as a treatment protocol.

Ayurveda also lays heavy emphasis on diet to produce a holistic effect, since different food items, as indicated below, differentially influence the doshas that constitute the body.

Also, the ayurvedic medications prescribed are a mixture of several compounds derived from natural sources, and work in a synergistic manner targeting different but coupled ailments simultaneously. This feature has the effect of minimising adverse side effects, which, on the other hand, are almost always encountered in allopathic treatments.

Few ayurvedic medications and their biological effects are listed below, as an illustration.

TASTE	Elements	Source examples	VĀTA	PITTA	KAPHA
SWEET (madhura)	Earth — Water	Honey, rice, sugar, fruit, carbohydrates, grains, natural sugars, milk	↓	↓	↑
SOUR (amla)	Earth — Fire	Yogurt, citrus fruits, ascorbic acid, vitamin C, vinegar, cheese, fermented foods	↓	↑	↑
SALTY (lavana)	Fire — Water	Seaweed, tamari, table salt, sea salt, sea vegetables	↓	↑	↑
PUNGENT (katu)	Air — Fire	Cayenne, chile pepper, black pepper, ginger, garlic, herbs and spices	↑	↑	↓
BITTER (tikta)	Air — Ether	Turmeric, dark leafy greens, herbs and spices	↑	↓	↓
ASTRINGENT (kashāya)	Air — Earth	Alum, green banana, legumes, raw fruits and vegetables, herbs	↑	↓	↓

Prashniparni

Vedic Medicine

अरायम् असृक्पावानं यश च स्फातिं जिहीर्षति ।
गर्भादे कण्वं नाशय पृष्निपर्णि सहस्व च ॥
अथर्व -२।२५।३॥

O' Prashniparni, help us in fight against all diseases that hampers body's growth, invites abortion and blood.

The Ayurvedic Pharmacopoeia of India recommends a decoction of whole plant in alcoholism, insanity, psyochosis; cough, bronchitis, dyspnoea; diseases due to vitiated blood; gout; bleeding piles; blood dysentery, acute diarrhoea.

The plant is credited with fracture-healing properties. Its total extract exhibits better and quicker healing of fractures in experimental animals due to early accumulation of phosphorus and more deposition of calcium.

triphala

The ayurvedic herbal fruit cocktail that heals/promotes health

Amalaki
Facilitates healthy
secretion of PITTA
in the GUT

Vibhitaki
Balances healthy
coating to KAPHA
in the GUT

Haritaki
Ensures healthy
movement of VATA
in the GUT

THEY SUPPORT NATURAL BODY FUNCTIONS SUCH AS:

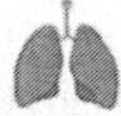

Liver

Respiratory System

Immune System

HEALTH BENEFITS OF TRIPHALA

Proper digestion, healthy
absorption, and assimilation
of nutrients, which is
essential for maintaining
a healthy body

Cleansing and
detoxification of
your body, which
will leave you
rejuvenated.

Cleansing of the
gastrointestinal
tract

Chapter 5

Soul, Super-Soul and Jagat

Summary: This chapter expands on the concepts briefly and qualitatively discussed in the chapter on spirituality, where the inferences on the abstract entities were derived primarily from the common daily experiences in life. The expanded description which supplements the life experiences is based on the scriptures, namely, the Vedas, which are accepted, by the most eminent philosophers and Acharyas, to be blemish-free, and hence invaluable guides for understanding those abstract entities at the fundamental level. Even so, there have been different interpretations of the Vedas, which have led to emergence of different philosophies.

IN the previous chapters I discussed the concepts of soul (also called Atma, Jeeva), super-soul (also called God, Paramatma, Brahman) and the world (also called as, 'jagat',, 'prithvi', 'bhulok' etc in different contexts), using exclusively logical and argumentative ways. A deeper question is regarding the relationship between these three entities. This is a topic which has been debated fiercely for several centuries and different philosophies have emerged as a consequence. Intriguingly, all these philosophies have flourished and continue to be followed by many groups. Interestingly, Lord Krishna, who is incarnation of Paramatma, gives a rationale to this situation in the Bhagavadgita in the following sloka:

ये यथा मां प्रपद्यन्ते तांस्तथैव भजाम्यहम् |
मम वर्त्मानुवर्तन्ते मनुष्याः पार्थ सर्वशः ||११||

BG 4.11: In whatever way people think of Me, I present myself to them in that manner. Everyone follows My path, knowingly or unknowingly, O son of Pritha.

Krishna also says in Bhagavadgita that there are various types of Jeevas, who, by common experience in this world, can be seen to be different from each other, and they naturally perceive him differently. Accordingly, their actions will also be different (Paramatma prompts them differently), which in turn, will result in the end, in different benefits or fruits.

Among the various philosophies some accept the Vedas as authentic scriptures, while others do not. There are also some philosophies which have emerged on the basis of individuals' experience and intellects. However, the most prominent among all of these are those which are based on the Vedas. The Vedas are very cryptic in Sanskrit thereby throwing up possibilities of different interpretations, and this has resulted in differences of convictions by different philosophers. Among these, three philosophies are most prominent, namely, Advaita (brought to prominence by Sri Adi Shankaracharya in the eighth century AD), Vishishtadvaita (propounded by Sri Ramanujacharya in the 10th century AD), and Dvaita (Propounded by Sri Madhwacharya in the 13th century AD). I have presented here the salient features of these three philosophies, with the limited knowledge that I have in all of these, in a simple narrative style, presenting at the same time some original supporting scriptures wherever possible. In a sense, Advaita, Vishishtadvaita and Dvaita, in that order, indicate the evolution of Vedantic philosophical thought over the centuries. Today, we do find followers of all the three philosophies. This must be generally attributed to individual inability to understand and decide on the abstract concepts and the tendency to go by affiliations to lineages.

Advaita Philosophy

Adhi Shankara

Adhi Shankaracharya is considered to be the incarnation of Shiva. He described Advaita philosophy by the following sloka.

ब्रह्म सत्यं जगन्मिथ्या जीवो ब्रह्मैव नापरः ।
अनेन वेद्यं सच्छास्त्रमिति वेदान्तडिण्डिमः ॥

Meaning: Brahman is real, the universe is mithya (it cannot be categorized as either real or unreal). The jeeva is Brahman itself and not different. This should be understood as the correct Sastra. This is the proclamation of Vedanta.

According to this philosophy, every soul is covered by a layer of ignorance and when this is removed by acquiring proper knowledge, the soul gets salvation and realizes that he/she is the God himself. This can happen even in his/her current life, or, if not, in a future life.

Advaita school believes that Brahman is the one and the only reality and everything else is a mere appearance, projection, formation or illusion (collectively termed as Maya). One of the most common examples used to describe the concept is, confusing of a rope for a snake when it is illuminated poorly. The rope on which snake was wrongly superimposed becomes evident when light comes on. The snake is an illusion, and the rope is the reality. In the same manner the world, animate and inanimate, appears in the mind because of its imposition over the Brahman. Another analogy given is that of a dream. In the dream a person sees various kinds of objects and once he wakes up he realizes that it was all untrue. So, this universe is likened to a dream. Getting liberation or moksha, which is the realisation that Brahman alone is real, after getting the proper knowledge is like waking up and coming out of the dream.

Further, Atman, the individual self, has no separate existence of his own. He is but a projection or reflection of Brahman only in each being. A Jeeva or Atma is a deluded Brahman by egoism, desires, and other impurities and thereby experiences duality and separation. Because of this each being is bound to the cycle of births and deaths and the laws of karma hold until liberation is achieved.

The world in which we live is a mere illusion, like a mirage. It appears in our consciousness because of the activity of the mind and the senses. Since we totally depend upon them, we do not perceive Brahman, the ultimate reality, who is hidden in all. When they are fully withdrawn and made silent through detachment, purity and renunciation, one can see the Supreme Self hidden in all and attain liberation.

Three levels of Reality

Notwithstanding the concept of *mithya* with regard to the universe, Shankaracharya introduced reality (Satya) at three levels:

(1) Praatibhasika Satya – This is illusory truth just like snake in place of the rope. This is shortlived.

(2) Vyavaharika Satya – This refers to day-to-day experiences involving Jeevas and Jagat (world). Here, he introduced the concept of Saguna Brahma who is Brahma with attributes (gunas) and who is responsible for all the activities in the universe. This has higher degree of reality and lasts for a longer time. Everything vanishes when Jeevas attain liberation after removal of ignorance or Avidya by receiving proper knowledge (Jnana) from Gurus and become one with the Parabrahma, the ultimate reality; Parabrahma is without any attributes (Nirguna)

(3) Paramarthika Satya – This is the ultimate reality.

Only Parabrahman belongs to this category. This is the only truth that exists for ever. The other two last only for limited durations.

Shankaracharya considered only some statements in the Vedas to be very relevant. These are popularly called as 'Mahavakyas'. These were said to indicate a fundamental principle (Tatwa) and hence were called as 'Tatwavedaka'. The many other statements in the Vedas which, in their opinion, either did not say anything that was not otherwise evident or gave information contradictory to the fundamental principle, were referred to as 'Atatwavedaka'.

Mahavakyas

The commonly quoted Mahavakyas are:

प्रज्ञानम् ब्रह्म | *Prajnanam Brahma,* Aitareya Upanishad 3.3, of Rig Veda

अयम् आत्मा ब्रह्म | *Ayam Atma Brahma,* Mandukya Upanishad 1.2, of Atharva Veda

तत् त्वम् असि | *Tat Tvam Asi,* Chandogya Upanishad 6.8.7, of Sama Veda, Kaivalya Upanishad

अहम् ब्रह्म अस्मि | *Aham Brahma Asmi,* Brihadaranyaka Upanishad 1.4.10, of Yajur Veda, Mahanarayana Upanishad

एकम् एव अद्वितीयं ब्रह्म- Brahman is one, without a second (Chāndogya Upaniṣad)

सोहम् - I am that (Isha Upanishad)

सर्वं खल्विदं ब्रह्म - All of this is brahman (Chāndogya Upaniṣad 3.14.1)

एतद्वै तत् - This, verily, is That (Katha Upanishad)

नेह नानास्ति किंचन – There is no diversity here (Katha Upanishad, Brihadaranyka Upanishad)

The meeting of Shankaracharya with Maharshi Vyasa who is incarnation of Bhagavan Vishnu.

Shankara's Bhashyas were put to severe test not only by the teachers of various schools of thought but also by the sage Vyasa himself. One day when Shankara on the banks of Ganges almost finished the day's class to his pupils, an old Brahmana appeared.

When told that Shankara has established a doctrine of non-dualism through his commentaries on Brahma Sutras, the old Brahmana sought Shankara's explanation on the various Sutras, and entered into a long debate extending over a number of days. After eight days, it struck Padmapada, the disciple of Shankaracharya that the Brahmana was none other than Vyasa, the very incarnation of Lord Vishnu and revealed this to Sri Shankara. Shankara prostrated before him and prayed for a candid opinion of his on the Bhashyas.

Sri Vyasa pleased with the request pronounced that Shankara with the help of the commentaries on Vedanta Sutras and many allied writings, would be able to refute all opposing doctrines and thereby become famous in the world.

Professors of philosophy in India refer to a verse from the *Padma Purana* (6.236.7) that reveals the hidden identity of Shankaracharya:

मायावादमसच्छास्त्रं प्रच्छन्नं बौद्ध उच्यते ।
मयैव कथितं देवि कलौ ब्राह्मणरूपिणा ॥७॥

"'The Mayavada philosophy,' Lord Shiva informed his wife Parvati, 'is covered Buddhism. In the form of a *brahmana* in the Kali-yuga I teach this imagined philosophy.'" Shankaracharya is thus widely accepted as an incarnation of Shiva.

Visishtadvaita Philosophy

Ramanujacharya

Ramanujacharya is considered to be the incarnation of Shesh-nag in Kaliyug. In his previous incarnation, i.e in Dwaparyug he was Balaram, the brother of Lord Krishna.

The Visishtadvaita system is an ancient one. It was originally expounded by Bodhayana in his Vritti, written around 400 B.C. It is the same as that is expounded by Ramanuja. Ramanuja followed Bodhayana in his interpretation of the Brahma Sutras. Ramanuja accepted the validity of all the Vedas and some other scriptures such as Pancharatra and the Puranas.

Ramanujacharya did not accept the views of Shankaracharya. According to him Brahman (Absolute reality), Jeeva and the world (Jagat) are all realities. He opposed the ideas of (1) invoking and distinguishing Saguna Brahman from Nirguna Brahma as the former was considered less than the latter, (2) Maya, (3) Vyavaharika Satya introduced by Shankaracharya.

The Brahman or the God

Visishtadvaita is called so because it inculcates the Advaita or oneness of Brahman, and Brahman has Visesha or attributes. It is, therefore, qualified monism. Brahman alone exists. All else that is seen are His manifestations or attributes. That is, Brahman of Sri Ramanuja is a complex organic whole—Visishta—though it is one. It admits plurality. Sri Ramanuja's Brahman or

Lord Narayana subsists in a plurality of forms as souls (Chit) and matter (Achit). These are related to Him as the body is related to the soul. They have no existence apart from Him. They inhere in Him as attributes in a substance. Matter and souls constitute the body of the Lord. The Lord is their in-dweller. He is the controlling Reality. Matter and souls are the subordinate elements. They are termed Viseshanas, attributes. God is the Viseshya or that which is qualified.

Ramanuja's Brahman is the all-powerful and all-wise Ruler of a real world, permeated and animated by His spirit. There is thus no room for the distinction between Param Nirguna Brahman and an Aparam Saguna Brahman whom advaitins referred to as Isvara. Ramanuja's Brahman is Savisesha Brahman, i.e., Brahman with attributes.

Brahman is omnipotent, omniscient and with infinite love. He is Saguna. When the Vedic texts declare that He is Nirguna, it means that there are no lower qualities such as sorrow, pain, mortality, change and old age in Him. He is full of auspicious attributes. He is of the nature of Satya (Truth), Jnana (Intelligence) and Ananda (Bliss). Matter and soul depend on Him. He is the Aadhara or support for this world and all souls. God is the Governor or Controller of the world. Jiva or soul is controlled by God.

Brahman is unchanging. The entire universe is latent in Him during Pralaya. The world is projected during creation, but this does not touch His essence. Ramanuja's Brahman has internal difference (Svagata Bheda). It is a synthetic whole, with souls and matter as Its modes (Chit-Achit-Visishta). The transcendent, the group, the incarnation, the image and the antaryamin are the five forms of the Lord.

Ramanuja identifies God with Narayana who dwells in Vaikuntha with His Sakti or consort, Lakshmi. Lakshmi is the Goddess of Prosperity. She is the Divine Mother. She pleads with Her husband on behalf of man. She introduces the devotee to Her Lord and obtains for him salvation. Lakshmi occupies a pre-eminent place in Vaishnavism.

The World or the Jagat

The world (Prakriti), with its variety of material forms of existence and individual souls, is not an unreal Maya, but a real part of Brahman's nature. It is the body of the Lord. Matter is real. It is

Achit or non-conscious substance. It undergoes a real Parinama or evolution. Matter exists in a subtle state as the Prakara of God during Pralaya. Hence it is eternal, but ever dependent. It is controlled by the will of God. It is neither good nor bad. It becomes a source of pleasure or of pain according to the nature of the Karma of souls. It forms the object of experience for the souls. Jagat, sometimes referred to as Prakriti has three Gunas: Sattva, Rajas and Tamas; but, Suddha-Tattva has only Sattva. It is pure matter. Suddha-Tattva is the substance which constitutes the body of God and is called His Nitya-Vibhuti. The manifested world is His Lila-Vibhuti.

The Soul or the Jeeva

The soul is a distinct individual entity and is a higher Prakara of God than matter, because it is a conscious entity. It is of the essence of God. According to Ramanuja, God, soul and Jagat are all eternal entities. The soul is self-conscious, unchanging, partless and atomic (Anu). The souls are infinite in number. The individual soul eternally distinct from God. It has indeed, sprung from Brahman, and is never outside Brahman; nevertheless, it enjoys a separate personal existence and will remain a personality forever.

According to Ramanuja, there are three classes of souls, viz., Nitya (eternal), Mukta (free) and Baddha (bound). Individual soul is a particle of which God is the whole. The eternal souls have never been in bondage. They are eternally free. They live with God in Vaikuntha. The freed souls were once subject to Samsara, but have attained salvation now and live with God. The bound souls are caught up in the meshes of Samsara and are striving to be released. They wander from life to life till they are redeemed.

When the individual soul is immersed in worldliness or Samsara, its knowledge is contracted. It gets its body according to its past Karma, and goes from birth to death and from death to birth, till it attains Moksha or the final emancipation. When it attains Moksha, its knowledge expands. It knows everything. "Every action that contracts the heart of the soul is bad, and every action that expands the heart of the soul is good"—this is the statement of Ramanuja. The soul is marching on in this Samsara, expanding or contracting through its good and evil actions, till it attains the final emancipation through the grace of Lord Narayana. The grace descends on those souls who are pure and struggling for the divine grace.

Moksha

According to Ramanuja, Moksha means the soul's passing from the troubles of mundane life into a kind of heaven or paradise (Vaikuntha) where it will remain forever in undisturbed personal bliss in the presence of God. The liberated soul attains the nature of God. But, it never becomes identical with Him. It lives in fellowship with the Lord, either serving Him or meditating on Him. It never loses its individuality. There is no such thing as Jivanmukti, according to Ramanuja. Salvation comes when the soul leaves the body. The final emancipation can be obtained only through Bhakti and the grace of the Lord. The grace of the Lord comes through devotion or absolute self-surrender. Karma and Jnana are only means to Bhakti.

Dvaita Philosophy

Madhwacharya is considered to be incarnation of Vayu. This is mentioned in Balitha Sukta (Rigveda) and Vayu purana. He is known by several other names: Purnaprajnya, Purnabodha,

Madhwacharya

प्रथमो हनुमान् नाम द्वितीयो भीम एवच ।
पूर्णप्रज्ञ तृतीयस्तु भगवत् कार्य साधकः ।।

Dashapramati, Anandatirtha, Sukhatirtha, are the most common ones.

अथ बळित्थासूक्तम्
(ऋग्वेद)

बळित्थेति पञ्चर्चस्य सूक्तस्य दीर्घतमा ऋषिः । वायुर्देवता । जगती छन्दः ।

बळित्था तद्वपुषे धायि दर्शतं देवस्य भर्गः सहसो यतो जनि ।
यदीमुप हरते साधते मतीर्ऋतस्य धेना अनयन्त ससुतः ।।१।।

पृक्षो वपुः पितुमान् नित्य आ शये द्वितीयमा सप्तशिवासु मातृषु ।
तृतीयमस्य वृषभस्य दोहसे दशप्रमतिं जनयन्त योषणः ।।२।।

निर्यदीं बुध्नान्महिषस्य वर्षस ईशानासः शवसा क्रन्त सूरयः ।
यदीमनु प्रदिवो मध्व आधवे गुहा सन्तं मातरिश्वा मथायति ।।३।।

प्र यत् पितुः परमान्नीयते पर्या पृक्षुधो वीरूधो दंसु रोहति ।
उभा यदस्य जनुषं यदिन्वत आदिद् यविष्ठो अभवद घृणा शुचिः ।।४।।

आदिन्मातृराविशद् याश्वा शुचिरहिंस्यमान उर्विया वि वावृधे ।
अनु यत् पूर्वा अरुहत् सनाजुवो नि नव्यसीष्ववरासु धावते ।।५।।

Here 'Dashapramati' in Shloka 2 and "Madhava" in Shloka 3 refers to Madhwacharya

Vayu puran

वायुर्दिव्यानि रूपाणी पञ्चत्रय शतानि च ।
त्रिकोटिमूर्त्ती संयुक्त त्रेतायां रक्षसांतकः ।
स "हनुमानिति" विख्यातो रामकार्य धुरन्दरः ।
स वामूर् "भीमसेनोपि" भू द्वापरान्ते कुरुद्धा।
कृष्णं संपूजयामास हत्वादुर्योधनादिकान् द्वैपायनस्य सेवार्थ
बदर्यातु कलौ युगे वायुश्च यति रूपेण कृत्वा दुश्शास्त्र
खण्डनम् । तथा कलियुगप्राप्ते तृतीयो "मध्व" नामकः भूरेके
दक्षिणभागे मणिमान् गर्व शान्तये ।।

Meaning: *lord Vayu has 3 crore Rupas in his Moola Roopa and is always at the service of lord Vishnu. In Treta Yuga lord Vayu took avatar as Hanuman to serve Rama and killed all the Raakshasa (demons). In Dwapara Yuga to serve lord Krishna Vayu took avatar as Bheemasena in kuru clan and killed the powerful demons like Duryodhana. in Kali Yuga lord Vayu took avatar as Madhvacharya in south India to serve Dwaipayana (Vedavyasa) and condemned all the dushshastra (wrong philosophy) and he crushed the ego of demon Maniman.*

As described in the later paragraphs, the Vedas mention about hierarchy in the abilities and knowledge levels of different devatas and among them Vayu is the highest. Thus, Madhwacharya was able to show that Vedas would get interpreted differently by different persons according to their 'yogyata' (intrinsic nature); there are three types of Jeevas: Satwik, Rajasik and Tamasik. Satwik Jeevas are the highest and Tamasic are the lowest in their intrinsic natures. In fact, maharshi Vedavyasa deliberately created such statements so that souls with different yogyatas will interpret them in a way that will take them to their respective ultimate destinations in the different kinds of heavens or the hells (Vaikuntha, Swarga, Naraka, Andhamtamas). Being the highest in terms of abilities, Madhwacharya was able to show the flaws in the interpretations by other Acharyas, even though they were also incarnations of some devatas.

Madhwacharya did not agree with both Shankaracharya and Ramanujacharya, although in many parts his views were similar to those of Ramanujacharya. He pointed out internal contradictions arising out of concepts of Maya, Vyavaharika Satya etc as promulgated by Shankaracharya. Simply put, if Maya is real it goes against the very Advaita Philosophy which claims that there is only one truth, and if it is unreal, then it is of no consequence. He demonstrated that the so-called 'mahavakyas' listed by Shankaracharya, when interpreted taking into consideration the contexts of their appearances in the Vedas or the Puranas, can be shown to be consistent with the thousands of other vakyas in the scriptures. His philosophy is termed as Dvaita Siddhanta. It is also referred to as philosophy of Dualism. He differed from Ramanujacharya on the status of the souls in the Moksha state and the nature of the Brahman himself (see below).

The philosophy of Madhwacharya is elegantly described by him in the *mangala sloka* of his work, **Mahabharat Tatparya Nirnaya**, as below.

नारायणाय परिपूर्ण गुणार्णवाय ।
विश्वोदयस्थितिलयोन्नियति प्रदाय ।
ज्ञानप्रदाय विबुधासुरसौख्य दुःख ।
सत्करणाय वितताय नमो नमस्ते ।

Meaning: Oh Lord Narayana, I bow to you again and again; you are like an ocean of infinite auspicious qualities [like knowledge and bliss], the originator and cause for the creation, sustenance, annihilation and primary instigator for the entire universe, bestower of knowledge [for uttamas, madhyamas and adhamas according to their yogyata], the highest cause for the inherent joy of gods (good people), inherent sorrow of demons (evil people) [by implication a mixture of joys and sorrow to the middle kind] and you pervade the universe in a unique and extra-ordinary way.

Shri Madhwacharya propounded the Dvaita siddhanta in the 13th century based on a self-consistent interpretation of the Vedas in their entirety. The Vedas are Nitya (eternal), Apourusheya (not manmade) and hence are blemish-free. Madhwacharya always had direct access to maharshi Vedavyasa, the incarnation of Paramatma himself, and hence his views are direct expressions of the Lord himself. As stated in Vayu Purana, Vayu took incarnation as Madhwa to refute wrong philosophies (Dusshyastra) and naturally, Madhwacharya was able to make a consistent interpretation of all the Vedas (unlike the advaitins who focused on a few statements (Mahavakyas) of the Vedas) and establish the ultimate truth pointing out the flaws in the interpretations by various other philosophers existing then, such as, Charvakas, Naiyyayikas, Vaisheshikas, Mimasakas, Bouddhhas, Sankhyas, Jains, Advaitins, Vishishtadvatinis, and others. This consistent interpretation of course demanded exemplary knowledge of vedic grammer and literature, sharpness and skill of giving proper context-dependent meanings to the seemingly contradictory phrases at different places in the Vedas. Madhwa Philosophy rests on two infallible pillars, namely, entire Vedas (Brahmasutras of Vedavyasa provide the basis for correct interpretation of the Vedas) and experiences of *chetanas*. He wrote 37 'Granthas' (philosophical works) which are now collectively called as 'Sarvamoola Granthas', and these present the Dvaita Philosophy, while at the same time point out the flaws in the other interpretations of the Vedas. The Unique feature of his works is that for every statement he makes he provides support (Pramana) from the Vedas and the Puranas which elaborate on the principles laid down in the Vedas. Madhwacharya also laid heavy emphasis on life experiences and hence his philosophy is also called as 'Philosophy of Realism'.

Soul, Jagat and Brahman (Paramatma)

The salient features of this Dvaita Siddhanta which may be termed as Madhwa Philosophy are as below.

1. The Universe or the world consists of Chetanas (Souls or Jeevas), Achetanas (matter which is referred to as Jada), and Brahman (Paramatma), who is very distinct from the other two.

2. The innumerable sentient and insentient objects we see around are not an illusion but are an absolute reality just like Paramatma. Every object has some attributes (e.g. whiteness of milk, flow of liquids etc.) which distinguish it from other objects and Madhwa alone declared that this property of separability is an intrinsic feature of the object (i.e non separable from the object) exactly like the other attributes, thereby avoiding infinite regress. Such coexistence of opposing attributes of non-separability and separability within objects is made possible by the attribute referred to as 'Vishesha'. This is a unique concept introduced by Madhwacharya.

3. Unlike the Jeeva and Jada components of the world, which are knowable through sense organs and logical arguments, Paramatma is knowable only through the Vedic texts. He is present both inside and outside the

world. He is the *paramachetana, eternal, omnipresent, sarvajnya, flawless (nirdosha), sarvaottama, anantagunapoorna, infinitely blissful, and achintya* (impossible for anybody to comprehend all His attributes). He is the, Creator (Srishti), Sustainer (sthiti) and Destroyer (Pralaya), and controls all actions of the chetanas in the world as a whole. He alone is functionally present through the Pralaya in all the cycles of creation and destruction. He is the only *sarvakartha,* and there is no job that He can't do, Further, Paramatma is totally *swatantra,* and does all this work without depending on any other chetana or achetana.

4. The entire universe resides inside Paramatma in a non-functional form during the Pralaya thereby maintaining nityatva of chetanas and achetanas. Srishti of the universe only means Paramatma gives the universe a functional form. Stithi means maintaining. Our dreams during sleep, which are created by Paramatma exemplify Srishti.

5. Though Paramatma takes various avtars, His abilities, characteristics remain identical in all these forms. This identity despite apparent

differences in the appearances is his Vishesha.

6. The dependence of souls (Jeeva) on Paramatma is total and eternal, and Madhwa describes Jeevas as Pratibimba (image) of Paramatma to illustrate this dependency. The so-called mirror (upadhi) creating the pratibimba can't be removed at any time, and therefore is identified to be intrinsic to the Jeeva as its vishesha. Other intrinsic attributes, namely, Ichha, Jnana and Kriya of jeevas are also their Visheshas.

7. There are five types of fundamental differences in the world (Panchabheda):

जीवेऽश्वर भिदा चैव जड़ेऽश्वर भिदा तथा ।
जीवभेदो मिथश्चैव जड़जीव भिदा तथा ।
मिथश्च जड़भेदोऽयं प्रपंच्यो भेद पंचकः ।।

-परमोपनिषद

Paramatma – Jeeva
Paramatma – Jada
Jeeva – Jeeva
Jeeva – Jada
Jada –Jada

Taratamya

8. There is a hierarchy (taratamya) among the Jeevas in their intrinsic *swaroopa*. This is referred to as *swabhava* or the *yogyata*. This is not changeable. This is an important point of difference from Vishishtadvaita. The following quote from Rig Veda explicitly describes this hierarchy.

सत्या विष्णोगुणाः सर्वे सत्या जीवेशयोर्भिदा ।
सत्यो मिधो जीवभेदः सत्यं च जगदीदृशम् ।।१.६८।।

असत्यः स्वागतो भेदो विष्णोर्नान्यदसत्यकम् ।
जगत् प्रवाहः सत्योऽयं पञ्चभेदसमन्वितः ।।१.६९।।

जीवेशयोर्भिदा चैव जीवभेदः परस्परम् ।
जडेशयोर्जडानां च जडजीवभिदा तथा ।।१.७०।।

पञ्चभेदा इमे नित्याः सर्वावस्थासु सर्वशः ।
मुक्तानां च हीयन्ते तारतम्यं च सर्वदा ।।१.७१।।

क्षितिपा मनुष्यगन्धर्वा दैवाश्च पितरश्चिराः ।
आजानजाः कर्मजाश्च देवा इन्द्रः पुरन्दरः ।।१.७२।।

रुद्रः सरस्वती वायुमुक्ताः शतगुणोत्तराः ।
एको ब्रह्मा च वायुश्च विन्द्रो रुद्रसमस्तथा ।
एको रुद्रस्तथा शेषो न कश्चिद वायुना समः ।।१.७३।।

मुक्तेषु श्रीस्तथा वायोः सहस्रगुणिता गुणैः ।
ततोऽनन्तगुणो विष्णुर्न कश्चित् तत्समः सदा ।।१.७४।।

1.68. All the attributes of Vishnu are true; the difference between the souls and the Lord is true, the difference between the souls inter se is true. This world of names, objects, deeds etc. is also true.

1.69. The only unreality is the supposed difference between Vishnu and His limbs, between Vishnu and His attributes, between Vishnu and His incarnations. Nothing else of the Lord is unreal. This eternal cycle of the universe consisting as it does of five essential differences is real, viz.,

1.70. (1) the difference between the Lord and the souls (2) the difference between the souls inter se (3) the difference between the Lord and matter (4) the difference between the matter inter se (5) the difference between the soul and matter.

1.71. These five differences are eternal, applicable at all times and conditions (of creation, destruction and sustenance). Neither these differences nor the gradations even among the released souls ever disappear.

1.72. Emperors, human gandharvas, Deva gandharvas, the ordinary Pitris, and the Chira Pitris, Ajanaja Devas (Devas by birth), Karma Devas (Devas by merit), Daksha, Indra, Rudra, Saraswathi and Vayu, all excel in merit the one next preceding by hundred counts.

1.73. Vayu and Brahma are equal. So also are Garuda and Rudra. Rudra and Sesha are similarly equal. There is none equal to Vayu, even among the released souls.

1.74. Lakshmi also excels Vayu in qualities counted thousand fold. Vishnu excels Her by infinite attributes. There is none ever equal to Him.

9. Among the Jeevas Vayu (equivalently four faced Brahma) is the highest followed by other Devatas, such as Garuda, Shesha, Rudra, Indra, Agni, Varuna, Yama, etc, and then Munis, Rishis etc. Vayu is therefore referred to as 'Jeevottama' and has naturally higher level of intellect and knowledge about Vedas, Vishnu and his Gunas than everybody else. That may be why he was able to find

flaws in the interpretations of the Vedas by Shankaracharya and Ramanujacharya. Here Brahma refers to Chaturmukha (four faced) Brahma who is the son of Vishnu.

10. Goddess Lakshmi, the consort of Paramatma is not among the Jeevas, stands above all the Jeevas, but she too is well below the Paramatma and under His control.

11. The Bimba-Pratibimba bhava follows the order in the hierarchy. At every step, the superior Jeeva is the bimba for the immediate next Jeeva in the hierarchy.

12. Every Jeeva has to go through the cycle of births and deaths. In every Janma, Jeeva gets a Prakrita sharira which is made up of matter (jada) as we see in this world. Sharira is necessary for carrying out actions (Karma).

13. Paramatma prompts, directs and controls at every step Jeeva's action (Karma) in every birth (Janma). He is the only *Swatantrakartha*. He gives karma phala (punya or papa) for every karma of the Jeeva as per the prescriptions in the Vedas (this will constitute Jeeva's Karmic account). Actions as per the prescriptions will give punya and those against will lead to papa. The prompts by the Paramatma at every

step will be as per the karmic account and swabhava of the Jeeva. The Vedas represent His Constitution. Only Paramatma is aware of the swabhava and karmic account of every Jeeva.

Moksha

14. Only Paramatma can give Moksha (liberation from the cycle of births and deaths) to the Jeevas. This will happen when the Karmic account is fully nullified. Papa will be destroyed and punya will be enjoyed.

15. The path to the Moksha of every Jeeva is predetermined, and may span several births, and this is determined by the swabhava and the karmic account of the individual Jeevas. There are basically two steps in the path to Moksha: Paroksha Jnana and Aparoksha Jnana.

16. Madhwacharya introduced the concept of Sakshi, which he defined as integral part of the Jeeva swaroopa. It is the Sakshi which acquires Jnana and also evaluates the validity (Pramanya) of the acquired jnana. Sakshi is also a Vishesha of the Jeeva.

17. Paroksha Jnana refers to knowledge from the

Vedas about the supremacy of the Paramatma, and dos and don'ts of Jeevas. Nishkama Karma free from attachment, and performed with a faith of absolute surrender to Paramatma are derivatives from the Paroksha Jnana.

18. Aparoksha Jnana refers to direct vision of the Paramatma in all His glory, as He wishes to show, after knowledge about the extraordinary attributes of Paramatma. After a Jeeva gets Aparoksha Jnana his Moksha is guaranteed, but this will actually be realised only after the karmic account is fully depleted and the so-called 'Prarabdha karma' is exhausted; this refers to the residual karma after Aparoksha Jnana. This can span through several births and while going through the Prarabdha karma, the jeeva does not acquire any more papa but acquires only punya. This happens by the desire of Paramatma and only to yogya Jeevas. At the end the Jeeva gets the Sakshatkara of his Bimba. Thus, different Jeevas comprehend Paramatma to different extents as per their Yogyata.

19. On the basis of swabhava, Jeevas are categorized into three types as 'Satvik', 'Rajasik' and 'Tamasik'. Only Satvik Jeevas

get Moksha, Rajasik are called Nitya Sansaris which means they keep revolving between Heaven, Hell and Bhulok. Tamasik Jeevas go permanently to Hell. In fact Paramatma directs every Jeeva in every birth in this context according to his swabhava.

20. Proper Jnana about Paramatma (His attributes and abilities, Mahatmya Jnana) leads to Devotion (Bhakti) which then leads to Bhagavatprasada, which in turn takes the Jeeva to his destination.

21. In the Moksha, the Jeevas are in their intrinsic forms with Aprakrita sharira, experience their intrinsic bliss the extent of which will be in accordance with their swabhava (Yogyata). They will be constantly in association with the Paramatma, yet distinctly different from him and under His control.

22. The hierarchy among the Jeevas persists in the Moksha state as well, unlike the view of Ramanujacharya.

Modern Science and Dvaita Philosophy

In Dvaita Philosophy the *World is real*. It is *Anadi, eternal and Savikara*. Every material object is called 'Jada'. There is a *Jada-Jada Bheda. Jada* can go through various transformations in size, shape, which is referred to as *Savikara.* But the total content is a constant (eternal). The body of a living species is also a Jada.

In Modern Science, *matter is real* and eternal. The various physical or chemical transformations that the matter goes through indicate it is *savikara.* For example, every atom is capable of undergoing a reaction which results in a new species (a molecule, for instance). Atom, or nucleus or electron can be converted into energy (photons) and vice-versa. Water can become ice or steam in a reversible manner. Solid metals can be melted in a reversible manner, etc.

The total content is unchangeable and constant (energy and matter put together), which means it is *eternal.*

Atoms, molecules etc can be counted, which means they are all separate entities. Avagodro's number (6.023×10^{23}) denoted as N, defines the number of atoms in one 'mole' of the substance (mole refers to the weight in gms equal to one Molecular Weight (MW) of the substance). For example, MW of water is 18, MW of hydrogen is 2, etc. So, 18 gms of water have N molecules of water. Even, in an ensemble of atoms or molecules of the same kind, every element is characterized by different physical property such as kinetic energy or potential energy and one talks of statistical property of the ensemble. All atoms in the Periodic Table are distinct entities. Therefore, materials made from these, individually, or by combination of two or more atom types are also clearly distinct. The DNA of living species is distinct, so much so that DNA test is used to identify a particular individual; the body of a living species is Jada.

Therefore, *Jada-Jada* Bheda is inherent to modern science.

Modern Science treats every object as real and physically existing and not as an illusion. This includes human bodies as well. One cannot do experiments with unreal objects. Notwithstanding, it must be mentioned that at the most fundamental level in modern science there is still a fair amount of confusion and uncertainty with regard to our understanding of the Universe and its creation.

Chapter 6

Philosophy of life

Summary: This chapter is basically a prescription for living a peaceful life in the modern world. The amazing developments in science and technology have on the one hand enhanced the comfort levels, but have also created an atmosphere of stress, on the other. The lifestyles have adversely affected relationships within families and in the society. This is due to the strong convictions that have evolved and the dwindling regard for spirituality perceived in a particular way. The chapter draws mostly from the Bhagavadgita to understand the causes of discomfort, stress, agony, sorrow, etc, and suggests steps to overcome these difficulties and lead a contented happy life and a harmonious society.

IN the background of what has been discussed in the previous chapters, some pertinent questions that come to every one's mind are: how to live the current life so as to be peaceful and happy? What should be the bottom line for our actions? What should be our aims and how do we achieve them? What are our dos and don'ts and our duties towards the society?

In this context, the first thing to remember is the relationship between the soul (jeevatma) and the super soul (Paramatma). This is stated explicitly below by taking messages from various scriptures, mostly from the Bhaghavadgita (BG) which is considered to be the essence of all Upanishads, and the teachings therein by Lord Krishna himself to Arjuna are most relevant to every human being, and these can be taken to represent the 'science of self-management' in life.

Both Jeevatma and Paramatma are eternal, but Jeevatma is always under the control of Paramatma. Body dies.

अविनाशि तु तद्विद्धि येन सर्वमिदं ततम् ।
विनाशमव्ययस्यास्य न कश्चित्कर्तुमर्हति ॥१७॥

BG 2.17: That which pervades the entire body, know it to be indestructible. No one can cause the destruction of the imperishable soul.

न जायते म्रियते वा कदाचिन्नायं भूत्वा भविता वा न भूयः ।
अजो नित्यः शाश्वतोऽयं पुराणो न हन्यते हन्यमाने शरीरे ॥२०॥

BG 2.20: The soul is neither born, nor does it ever die; nor having once existed, does it ever cease to be. The soul is without birth, eternal, immortal, and ageless. It is not destroyed when the body is destroyed.

वासांसि जीर्णानि यथा विहाय नवानि गृह्णाति नरोऽपराणि ।
तथा शरीराणि विहाय जीर्णान्यन्यानि संयाति नवानि देही ॥२२॥

BG 2.22: As a person sheds worn-out garments and wears new ones, likewise, at the time of death, the soul casts off its worn-out body and enters a new one.

मत्तः परतरं नान्यत्किञ्चिदस्ति धनञ्जय ।
मयि सर्वमिदं प्रोतं सूत्रे मणिगणा इव ॥७॥

BG 7.7: There is nothing higher than Myself, O Arjun. Everything rests in Me, as beads strung on a thread.

कर्मण्येवाधिकारस्ते मा फलेषु कदाचन ।
मा कर्मफलहेतुर्भूर्मा ते सङ्गोऽस्त्वकर्मणि ॥४७॥

BG 2.47: You have a right to perform your prescribed duties, but you have no control over the fruits of your actions. Never consider yourself to be the cause of the results of your activities, nor be attached to inaction.

नियतं सङ्गरहितमरागद्वेषतः कृतम् ।
अफलप्रेप्सुना कर्म यत्तत्सात्त्विकमुच्यते ॥२३॥

BG 18.23: Action that is in accordance with the scriptures, which is free from attachment and aversion, and which is done without desire for rewards, is in the mode of goodness. **(Punya Karma)**

अनुबन्धं क्षयं हिंसामनपेक्ष्य च पौरुषम् ।
मोहादारभ्यते कर्म यत्तत्तामसमुच्यते ॥२५॥

BG 18.25: That action is declared to be in the mode of ignorance, which is begun out of delusion, without thought to one's own ability, and disregarding consequences, loss, and injury to others **(Papa Karma)**.

ध्यायतो विषयान्पुंसः सङ्गस्तेषूपजायते ।
सङ्गात्सञ्जायते कामः कामात्क्रोधोऽभिजायते ॥६२॥

BG 2.62: While contemplating on the objects of the senses, one develops attachment to them. Attachment leads to desire, and from desire arises anger.

क्रोधान्द्रवति सम्मोहः सम्मोहात्स्मृतिविभ्रमः ।
स्मृतिभ्रंशाद्बुद्धिनाशो बुद्धिनाशात्प्रणश्यति ॥६३॥

BG 2.63 From anger, delusion arises, and from delusion bewilderment of memory. When memory is bewildered, intelligence is lost, and when intelligence is lost, he destroys himself.

प्रजहाति यदा कामान्सर्वान्पार्थ मनोगतान् ।
आत्मन्येवात्मना तुष्टः स्थितप्रज्ञस्तदोच्यते ॥५५॥

BG 2.55: The Supreme Lord said: O Parth, when one discards all selfish desires and cravings of the senses that torment the mind, and becomes satisfied in the realization of the self, such a person is said to be transcendentally situated.

Lord Krishna has given the prescription to become a *Sthitaprajna*. He is an individual who has conquered the common enemies of a human being, namely, arrogance, jealousy, attachment, greed, anger, desires. Such a person will be happy and leads a peaceful life.

रागद्वेषविमुक्तैस्तु विषयनिन्द्रियैश्चरन् ।
आत्मवश्यैर्विधेयात्मा प्रसादमधिगच्छति ॥६४॥

BG 2.64: One who controls the mind, and is free from attachment and aversion, even while using

the objects of the senses, attains the Grace of God
(Punya phala).

प्रसादे सर्वदुःखानां हानिरस्योपजायते ।
प्रसन्नचेतसो ह्याशु बुद्धिः पर्यवतिष्ठते ॥६५॥

*BG 2.65: By divine grace comes the peace in which
all sorrows end, and the intellect of such a person
of tranquil mind soon becomes firmly established in
God* **(Punya phala)**.

सर्वस्य चाहं हृदि सन्निविष्टो
मत्तः स्मृतिर्ज्ञानमपोहनं च ।
वेदैश्च सर्वैरहमेव वेद्यो
वेदान्तकृद्वेदविदेव चाहम् ॥१५॥

*BG 15.15: I am seated in the hearts of all living
beings, and from Me come memory, knowledge, as
well as forgetfulness. I alone am to be known by all
the Vedas, am the author of the Vedant, and the
knower of the meaning of the Vedas.*

द्वाविमौ पुरुषौ लोके क्षरश्चाक्षर एव च ।
क्षरः सर्वाणि भूतानि कूटस्थोऽक्षर उच्यते ॥१६॥

*BG 15.16: There are two kinds of beings in creation,
the kṣhar (perishable) and the akṣhar (imperishable).
The perishable are all beings in the material realm.
The imperishable are the the liberated beings.*

उत्तमः पुरुषस्त्वन्यः परमात्मेत्युदाहतः |
यो लोकत्रयमाविश्य बिभर्त्यव्यय ईश्वरः ||१७||

BG 15.17: Besides these, is the Supreme Divine Personality, who is the indestructible Supreme Soul. He enters the three worlds as the unchanging Controller and supports all living beings.

यस्मात्क्षरमतीतोऽहमक्षरादपि चोत्तमः |
अतोऽस्मि लोके वेदे च प्रथितः पुरुषोत्तमः ||१८||

BG 15.18: I am transcendental to the perishable world of matter, and even to the imperishable soul; hence I am celebrated, both in the Vedas and the Smṛitis, as the Supreme Divine Personality.

यो मामेवमसम्मूढो जानाति पुरुषोत्तमम् |
स सर्वविद्भजति मां सर्वभावेन भारत ||१९||

BG 15.19: Those who know Me without doubt as the Supreme Divine Personality truly have complete knowledge. O Arjun, they worship Me with their whole being.

The Supreme Lord is situated as Paramātmā in everyone›s heart, and it is by Him that all activities are initiated. The living entity forgets everything of his past life, but he has to act according to the direction of the Supreme Lord, who is witness to all his work. Therefore he begins his work according to his past deeds. Required knowledge is supplied to him, and remembrance is given to him, and he forgets, also, about his past life. Thus, the Lord is not only all-pervading; He is also localized in every individual heart. He awards the different fruitive results. He is not only worshippable as the impersonal Brahman, the Supreme Personality of Godhead, and the localized Paramātmā, but as the form of the incarnation of the *Vedas* as well. The *Vedas* give the right direction to the people. The *Vedas* offer knowledge of the Supreme GOD. His incarnation as Vedavyas is the compiler of the Brahma sūtra. God's power is summarily described by the following commonly cited Sanskrit statement.

तेन विना तृणमपि न चलति।

Without Him, even a single grass cannot move

नैव किञ्चित्करोमीति युक्तो मन्येत तत्त्ववित् ।
पश्यञ्शृण्वन्स्पृशञ्जिघ्रन्नश्नन्गच्छन्स्वपन्श्वसन् ॥८॥
प्रलपन्विसृजन्गृह्णन्नुन्मिषन्निमिषन्नपि ।
इन्द्रियाणीन्द्रियार्थेषु वर्तन्त इति धारयन् ॥९॥

BG 5.8-9: Those steadfast in karm yog, always think, "I am not the doer," even while engaged in seeing, hearing, touching, smelling, moving, sleeping, breathing, speaking, excreting, grasping, and opening or closing the eyes. With the light of divine knowledge, they see that it is only the material senses that are moving amongst their objects.

प्रकृतेः क्रियमाणानि गुणैः कर्माणि सर्वशः |
अहङ्कारविमूढात्मा कर्ताहमिति मन्यते ||२७||

BG 3.27: All activities are carried out by the three modes of material nature. But in ignorance, the soul, deluded by false identification with the body, thinks of itself as the doer.

The person in material consciousness is convinced by false ego that he is the doer of everything. He does not know that the mechanism of the body is produced by material nature, which works under the supervision of the Supreme Lord. The materialistic person has no knowledge that ultimately he is under the control of Krishna. The person in false ego takes all credit for doing everything independently, and that is the symptom of his nescience.

What did Madhwacharya, the incarnation of Vayu, the son of GOD, say?

नाहं कर्ता हरिः कर्ता तत्पूजा कर्म चाखिळम् ।
तथाऽपि मत्कृता पूजा तत्प्रसादेन नान्यथा ।।

Meaning: *I am not the doer, Shri Hari is the doer, all the actions that I do are His worship. Even then, the worshiop I do is through His grace and not otherwise. That devotion and the fruits of the actions that come to me are due to His recurring grace.*

Paramatma resides in the body of every soul, makes him do Karma using the body which He has given to the soul, gives phala as per the Karma – Phala relationship prescribed in the Vedas. Good Karma (satkarma) represents Dharma and bad karma (Duskarma) represents Adharma. Satkarma is Punya which yields Sukh, while Dushkarma is Papa which yields Dukh. God makes soul experience the phala in the form of Sukh (Hapiness) or Dukh (Miseries).

Paramatma gives the soul memory and forgetfulness alike, gives him knowledge of the reality. Through his Maya Paramatma also clouds the intellect of all souls (except Vayu) and even the great rishis can occasionally get affected, and think that they are the doers, but this ignorance is very short-lived in them and they immediately reconcile. Paramatma may at times engage them to do wrong karma to achieve some other objective. Here, the rishis or other devtas are his instruments. They are called 'Bhagavadkarya sadhaka'. There are many incidents like this described in the Puranas.

There are three intrinsically different (Swabhava or Yogyata) groups of souls: Satvik, Rajas, Tamas. Satvik is the highest category (all devtas belong here) and Tamas is the lowest category (all asuras belong here). Rajas are the middle category. In each category there are innumerable number of souls who are all different from each other. God does not change the intrinsic natures of the souls.

Their ultimate destinations at the end of the cycle of births and deaths are also different and they have different levels of Sukh (Happiness). The journey of every soul to the ultimate destination is like traveling in a train with many stations which represent the different births. The compartment represents the Samsara or the karmic experiences in every life.

Paramatma (driver in the engine of the train) takes every soul to his ultimate destination with well-defined extent of Sukh or Dukh: Vaikuntha has only Sukh and Andhantamas has only Dukh.

There are intermediate states also.

Only He knows the path to their respective destinations and accordingly He creates situations for punya karma (which gives sukh) and papa karma (which gives dukh). He controls the intellect and prompts soul's actions. In this context, He guides the ignorant soul through a teacher who advises for the actions to be taken at every step; so, the teacher is called **Bhagavadkarya sadhaka**.

Which is good karma and which is bad karma is context dependent. In other words, Dharma and Adharma will be context dependent. For example, killing an Asura who is destructor of the Society, is not Adharma. Lord Krishna himself says,

परित्राणाय साधूनां विनाशाय च दुष्कृताम् |
धर्मसंस्थापनार्थाय सम्भवामि युगे युगे ||८||

BG 4.8: To protect the righteous, to annihilate the wicked, and to reestablish the principles of dharma I appear on this earth, age after age.

In this endeavour Paramatma engages many **Bhagavadkarya sadhakas.** For example, in Mahabharat, Draupadi was his instrument to destroy all Kauravas who, by nature were Adharmi. He prompted them to do all papa karma against Draupadi and her husbands who were Dharmic people and his devotees. We find innumerable examples of such incidents in our puranas. These are described in the Vedashastras where the responsibilities, the dos and don'ts for different categories of people (Brahmana, Kshatriya, Vaishya, Shudra – this is sharing of responsibilities) are explicitly mentioned, and that is where the need to study shastras arises. As the soul loses his ignorance, gains knowledge, he will start appreciating the greatness of GOD, will become thankful to GOD for everything and then reaches the state of ultimate bliss, the Moksha. Thus, the path to the ultimate destination for every soul is: Karma – Jnana – Moksha.

Take home lesson for the ignorant soul

- Recognise that GOD (Paramatma) is the Supreme Commander, Sarvajnya, all pervasive, dictates every one's intellect.
- Shed the ego and recognise that every individual is performing Karma in every life as desired by GOD. GOD prompts at every step and hence success and failures are in His control.

- Try and understand the subtleties of Dharma and Adharma by learning Shastras through a Guru.
- Remember that GOD always protects Dharma and His devotees who recognise His greatness and dedicate everything they do or achieve at His feet.
- GOD creates situations for every soul in every life to facilitate his journey towards his ultimate destination. He gives happiness or sorrow as may be required at different stages of the journey.
- Recognise that all souls are different and avoid making unnecessary comparisons and create futile ambitions.
- Shed anger, jealousy, arrogance, greed, and be peaceful.
- Reading Vedashashtras through a Guru and living a life as per the prescription of the shashtras is essential to reach a state of permanent bliss

In the end, I submit this at the feet of the Almighty, Paramatma, who prompted, guided, and enabled me by providing physical and intellectual strength in producing this work. I do hope, this will benefit the readers.

Chapter 7

Shanti

(Peace) Veda mantras and Bhagavadgita

ॐ शं नो मित्रः शं वरुणः।

शं नो भवत्वर्यमा।

शं न इन्द्रो बृहस्पतिः।

शं नो विष्णुरुरुक्रमः।

नमो ब्रह्मणे।

नमस्ते वायो।

त्वमेव प्रत्यक्षं ब्रह्मासि।

त्वामेव प्रत्यक्षम् ब्रह्म वदिष्यामि।

ऋतं वदिष्यामि।

सत्यं वदिष्यामि।

तन्मामवतु।

तद्वक्तारमवतु।

अवतु माम्।

अवतु वक्तारम्।

ॐ शान्तिः शान्तिः शान्तिः॥

Om May Mitra be blissful to us.

May Varuna be blissful to us.

May Aryaman be blissful to us.

May Indra and Brihaspati be blissful to us.

May Vishnu, of long strides, be blissful to us.

Salutation to Brahman.

Salutation to you, O Vayu.

You, indeed, are the immediate Brahman.

You alone I shall call the direct Brahman.

I shall call you righteousness. I shall call you truth.

May He protect me.

May He protect the reciter*.

May He protect me.

May He protect the reciter.

Om, peace, peace, peace

ॐ सह नाववतु ।
सह नौ भुनक्तु ।
सह वीर्यं करवावहै ।
तेजस्वि नावधीतमस्तु मा विद्विषावहै ।
ॐ शान्तिः शान्तिः शान्तिः ।।

Meaning:

1. *Om, Together may we two Move (in our studies, the Teacher and the Student),*

2. *Together may we two Relish (our Studies, the Teacher and the Student),*

3. *Together may we perform (our studies) with Vigour (with deep Concentration),*

4. *May what has been studied by us be filled with the Brilliance (of Understanding, leading to knowledge); May it Not give rise to Hostility (due to lack of Understanding),*

5. *Om, Peace, Peace, Peace.*

अनन्याश्चिन्तयन्तो मां ये जनाः पर्युपासते ।
तेषां नित्याभियुक्तानां योगक्षेमंवहाम्यहम् ।।२२।।

Meaning: *There are those who always think of Me and engage in exclusive devotion to Me. To them, whose minds are always absorbed in Me, I provide what they lack and preserve what they already possess.*

ॐ सर्वे भवन्तु सुखिनः ।
सर्वे सन्तु निरामयाः ।
सर्वे भद्राणि पश्यन्तु
मा कश्चिद् दुःख भाग्भवेत्
ॐ शान्तिः शान्तिः शान्तिः ।।

Meaning:

1.   *Om, May All be Happy,*
2.   *May All be Free from Illness.*
3.   *May All See what is Auspicious,*
4.   *May no one Suffer.*
5.   *Om, Peace, Peace, Peace.*

ॐ सर्वेषां स्वस्तिर्भवतु ।
सर्वेषां शान्तिर्भवतु ।
सर्वेषां पूर्णंभवतु ।
सर्वेषां मंङ्गलंभवतु ।
ॐ शान्तिः शान्तिः शान्तिः ।।

Meaning:

1.   *May there be Well-Being in All,*
2.   *May there be Peace in All,*
3.   *May there be Fulfilment in All,*
4.   *May there be Auspiciousness in All,*
5.   *Om, Peace, Peace, Peace.*

ॐ असतो मा सद् गमय ।
तमसो मा ज्योतिर्गमय ।
मृत्योर्मा अमृतं गमय ।
ॐ शान्तिः शान्तिः शान्तिः ।।

Meaning:

1. *Om, (O Lord) From (the Phenomenal World of) Unreality, make me go (i.e. Lead me) towards the Reality (of Eternal Self),*

2. *From Darkness (of Ignorance), make me go (i.e. Lead me towards the Light (of Spritual Knowledge),*

3. *From (the World of) Mortality (of Material Attachment), make me go (i.e. Lead me) towards the World of Immortality (of Self-Realization),*

4. *Om, Peace, Peace, Peace.*

ॐ दयौः शान्तिरन्तरिक्षं शान्तिः ।
पृथ्वी शान्तिरापः शान्तिरोषधयः शान्तिः ।
वनसपतयः शान्तिर्विश्वेदेवाः शान्तिर्ब्रह्म शान्तिः ।
सर्व शान्तिः शान्तिरेव शान्तिः सा मा शान्तिरेध ।।
ॐ शान्तिः शान्तिः शान्तिः ।।

Meaning:

1. *Om, Peace is in Sky; Peace is in Space (between Earth and Sky);*

2. *Peace is in Earth; Peace is in Water; Peace is Plants;*

3. *Peace is in Trees; Peace is in Gods (presiding over various elements of Nature); Peace is in Brahman (absolute Consciousness);*

4. *Peace is pervading everywhere; Peace alone (which is outside) is in Peace (which is inside); May you be (established in) that Peace (and make your life fulfilled);*

5. *Om, Peace, Peace, Peace.*

About the Author

Ramakrishna Vijayacharya Hosur (b. 1953), had his school education in Dharwad (Karanataka), received M.Sc. (Chemistry) from Indian Institute of Technology (IIT), Bombay in 1973 and Ph.D. (Chemistry) from Tata Institute of Fundamental Research (TIFR, affiliated to University of Mumbai) in 1979. He was post-doctoral fellow at ETH Zürich, Switzerland

(1981-83) in the group of Prof. Kurt Wüthrich and also collaborated with Prof. Richard Ernst. Prof. Ernst was awarded Nobel Prize in Chemistry in 1991 and Prof. Wüthrich was also awarded Nobel Prize in Chemistry in 2002. He has been employed at TIFR since 1978, and retired as Senior Professor in May 2018. He was also Director of the University of Mumbai (UM) – Department of Atomic Energy (DAE) Centre for Excellence in Basic Sciences (CEBS) from December 2009 till October 2017. He was the Convener of the National Facility for High Field NMR at TIFR during 2002-2018. Currently, he is associated with CEBS and also with Indian Institute of Technology (IIT) - Bombay. His research has been in the area of Nuclear Magnetic Resonance (NMR) and its applications in chemistry and biology over the last four decades. He is an author of nearly 300 scientific research publications and four books and several book chapters relating to scientific work. He has been an invited speaker at many National and International conferences in India and abroad.

The author's work has been recognized by several awards, such as Young Scientist Medal of the Indian National Science Academy, BM Birla Award, GN Ramachandran Gold Medal of CSIR, Govt of India, JC Bose National Fellowship, CL Khetrapal Award, to name a few. He has been awarded 'Padmashri' by the President of India in 2014. He is an elected Fellow of International Society of Magnetic Resonance (ISMAR), The World Academy of Sciences (TWAS), and all the Science Academies of India.

The author has deep interest in philosophy to which he got introduced by his grandfather, Shri Vidyaratna R. S. Panchamukhi, who was an extraordinary scholar in Sanskrit language and philosophy, an author of nearly 150 books on various topics reflecting ancient wisdom in India, and a recipient of President's Medal for his contributions. The author's family has a great tradition of philosophy and religion, on one hand, and modern education on the other. While pursuing his profession as a scientist, he also learnt Sanskrit language by reading various kaavyas and plays written by great poets and writers. Simultaneously, he learnt some aspects of Philosophy, especially, Vedanta, from various Acharyas and maternal uncles, Dr. V. R. Panchamukhi and Dr. P. R. Panchamukhi.

Message

The relationship between Science and Spirituality is a topic of great interest to most people, and, therefore, continues to be debated fiercely in both scientific and spiritual circles. The author, who is recognized as an expert in both fields, has tried to show that Science and Spirituality are inseparable and are complementary. The book progresses systematically in building up the narrative, by first showing the glorious developments in science, and then relies on irrefutable common experiences in life to establish the fundamental concepts in spiritualty of Consciousness (Soul or Atma), Super-soul (God or Paramatma), Order, and such other entities that are not amenable to experimentation. Both Science and Spirituality have the same objective, namely, bring success, peace and happiness in everyone's life. A peaceful mind will be more receptive and more creative, and thus will be able to achieve greater scientific discoveries and feats which would enhance the quality of life and benefit mankind, in general. The author consolidates this position further by drawing from the ancient wisdom, with regard to creation of the Universe, Order in the Universe and health aspects. Delving deeper into the philosophical concepts the author demonstrates the 'inclusivity of different schools of thoughts' inherent in Spirituality. In all of this discussion Sanskrit statements from original scriptures are cited to establish the authenticity, but their meanings in English are also included for easy comprehension. The spiritual texts also give prescriptions for a happy life, which we may call as 'Science of Self-management' or 'Philosophy of Life'.

The book is a good read, and motivates one and all for a virtuous living and a peaceful life.

Dr. Madhusoodan V Hosur
Former Head, Protein Crystallography Section
Solid State Physics Division,
Bhabha Atomic Research Centre (BARC), Mumbai